Fix-It and Forget-It

SLOW COOKER

Comfort Foods

150 HEALTHY AND NUTRITIOUS RECIPES

HOPE COMERFORD

Photos by Bonnie Matthews

Good Books

New York, New York

Table of Contents

Welcome to Fix-It and Forget-It Slow Cooker Comfort Foods

Comfort foods are the foods that remind of us our childhood, a special memory, or special moments. They are the foods we want when we're feeling down or craving a visit "home." They're not always the "healthiest" foods though, so that is where this book comes in! I've tried to choose 150 recipes for you that satisfy those "comfort food" cravings without the guilt! So, fire up the slow cooker and give yourself a warm hug from the inside out!

This book is divided into five different categories for you: Breakfasts, Soups, Stews & Chilies, Main Dishes, Side Dishes & Vegetables, and Desserts. For every recipe, we've included nutritional information to further help you with your dietary needs.

If you find a recipe you love, but it calls for an ingredient you can't have, please feel free to sub it with one that fits your particular allergen or dietary needs. For instance, if a recipe calls for peanut butter, but you have a peanut allergy, feel free to replace it with sunflower butter. It's easy to make a recipe work for you! Most of the recipes in this book can be very easily adjusted.

Choosing a Slow Cooker

Not all slow cookers are created equal . . . or work equally as well for everyone!

Those of us who use slow cookers frequently know we have our own preferences when it comes to which slow cooker we choose to use. For instance, I love my programmable slow cooker, but there are many programmable slow cookers I've tried that I've strongly disliked. Why? Because some go by increments of 15 or 30 minutes and some go by 4, 6, 8, or 10 hours. I dislike those restrictions, but I have family and friends who don't mind them at all! I am also pretty brand loyal when it comes to my manual slow cookers because I've had great success with those and have had unsuccessful moments with slow cookers of other brands. So, which slow cooker(s) is/are best for your household?

It really depends on how many people you're feeding and if you're gone for long periods of time. Here are my recommendations:

For 2–3 person household	3–5 quart slow cooker
For 4–5 person household	5–6 quart slow cooker
For a 6+ person household	6½–7 quart slow cooker

Large slow cooker advantages/disadvantages:

Advantages:
- You can fit a loaf pan or a baking dish into a 6- or 7-quart, depending on the shape of your cooker. That allows you to make bread or cakes, or even smaller quantities of main dishes. (Take your favorite baking dish and loaf pan along when you shop for a cooker to make sure they'll fit inside.)
- You can feed large groups of people, or make larger quantities of food, allowing for leftovers, or meals, to freeze.

Disadvantages:
- They take up more storage room.
- They don't fit as neatly into a dishwasher.
- If your crock isn't ⅔–¾ full, you may burn your food.

Small slow cooker advantages/disadvantages:

Advantages:
- They're great for lots of appetizers, for serving hot drinks, for baking cakes straight in the crock, and for dorm rooms or apartments.
- Great option for making recipes of smaller quantities.

Disadvantages:
- Food in smaller quantities tends to cook more quickly than larger amounts. So keep an eye on it.
- Chances are, you won't have many leftovers. So, if you like to have leftovers, a smaller slow cooker may not be a good option for you.

My recommendation:

Have at least two slow cookers; one around 3 to 4 quarts and one 6 quarts or larger. A third would be a huge bonus (and a great advantage to your cooking repertoire!). The advantage of having at least a couple is you can make a larger variety of recipes. Also, you can make at least two or three dishes at once for a whole meal.

Manual vs. Programmable

If you are gone for only six to eight hours a day, a manual slow cooker might be just fine for you. If you are gone for more than eight hours during the day, I would highly recommend purchasing a programmable slow cooker that will switch to warm when the cook time you set is up. It will allow you to cook a wider variety of recipes.

The two I use most frequently are my 4-quart manual slow cooker and my 6½-quart programmable slow cooker. I like that I can make smaller portions in my 4-quart slow cooker on days I don't need or want leftovers, but I also love how my 6½-quart slow cooker can accommodate whole chickens, turkey breasts, hams, or big batches of soups. I use them both often.

Get to know your slow cooker . . .

Plan a little time to get acquainted with your slow cooker. Each slow cooker has its own personality—just like your oven (and your car). Plus, many new slow cookers cook hotter and faster than earlier models. I think that with all of the concern for food safety, the slow-cooker manufacturers have amped up their settings so that "High," "Low," and "Warm" are all higher temperatures than in the older models. That means they cook hotter—and therefore, faster—than the first slow cookers. The beauty of these little machines is that they're supposed to cook low and slow. We count on that when we flip the switch in the morning before we leave the house for ten hours or so. So, because none of us knows what kind of temperament our slow cooker has until we try it out, nor how hot it cooks—don't assume anything. Save yourself a disappointment and make the first recipe in your new slow cooker on a day when you're at home. Cook it for the shortest amount of time the recipe calls for. Then, check the food to see if it's done. Or if you start smelling food that seems to be finished, turn off the cooker and rescue your food.

Also, all slow cookers seem to have a "hot spot," which is of great importance to know, especially when baking with your slow cooker. This spot may tend to burn food in that area if you're not careful. If you're baking directly in your slow cooker, I recommend covering the "hot spot" with some foil.

Take notes . . .

Don't be afraid to make notes in your cookbook. It's yours! Chances are, it will eventually get passed down to someone in your family and they will love and appreciate all of your musings. Take note of which slow cooker you used and exactly how long it took to cook the recipe. The next time you make it, you won't need to try to remember. Apply what you learned to the next recipes you make in your cooker. If another recipe says it needs to cook 7–9 hours, and you've discovered your slow cooker cooks on the faster side, cook that recipe for 6–6½ hours and then check it. You can always cook a recipe longer—but you can't reverse things if it's overdone.

Get creative . . .

If you know your morning is going to be hectic, prepare everything the night before, take it out so the crock warms up to room temperature when you first get up in the morning, then plug it in and turn it on as you're leaving the house.

   If you want to make something that has a short cook time and you're going to be gone longer than that, cook it the night before and refrigerate it for the next day. Warm it up when you get home. Or, cook those recipes on the weekend when you know you'll be home and eat them later in the week.

Slow Cooking Tips and Tricks and Other Things You May Not Know

- Slow cookers tend to work best when they're ⅔ to ¾ of the way full. You may need to increase the cooking time if you've exceeded that amount, or reduce it if you've put in less than that. If you're going to exceed that limit, it would be best to reduce the recipe, or split it between two slow cookers. (Remember how I suggested owning at least two or three slow cookers?)

- Keep your veggies on the bottom. That puts them in more direct contact with the heat. The fuller your slow cooker, the longer it will take its contents to cook. Also, the more densely packed the cooker's contents are, the longer they will take to cook. And finally, the larger the chunks of meat or vegetables, the more time they will need to cook.

- Keep the lid on! Every time you take a peek, you lose 20 minutes of cooking time. Please take this into consideration each time you lift the lid! I know, some of you can't help yourself and are going to lift anyway. Just don't forget to tack on 20 minutes to your cook time for each time you peeked!

- Sometimes it's beneficial to remove the lid. If you'd like your dish to thicken a bit, take the lid off during the last half hour to hour of cooking time.

- If you have a big slow cooker (7- to 8-quart), you can cook a small batch in it by putting the recipe ingredients into an oven-safe baking dish or baking pan and then placing that into the cooker's crock. First, put a trivet or some metal jar rings on the bottom of the crock, and then set your dish or pan on top of them. Or a loaf pan may "hook onto" the top ridges of the crock belonging to a large oval cooker and hang there straight and securely, "baking" a cake or quick bread. Cover the cooker and flip it on.

- The outside of your slow cooker will be hot! Please remember to keep it out of reach of children and keep that in mind for yourself as well!
- Get yourself a quick-read meat thermometer and use it! This helps remove the question of whether or not your meat is fully cooked, and helps prevent you from overcooking your meat as well.

Internal Cooking Temperatures:
  - Beef—125–130°F (rare); 140–145°F (medium); 160°F (well-done)
  - Pork—140–145°F (rare); 145–150°F (medium); 160°F (well-done)
  - Turkey and Chicken—165°F
  - Frozen Meat: The basic rule of thumb is, don't put frozen meat into the slow cooker. The meat does not reach the proper internal temperature in time. This especially applies to thick cuts of meat! Proceed with caution!
- Add fresh herbs 10 minutes before the end of the cooking time to maximize their flavor.
- If your recipe calls for cooked pasta, add it 10 minutes before the end of the cooking time if the cooker is on High; 30 minutes before the end of the cooking time if it's on Low. Then the pasta won't get mushy.
- If your recipe calls for sour cream or cream, stir it in 5 minutes before the end of the cooking time. You want it to heat but not boil or simmer.

Approximate Slow Cooker Temperatures (Remember, each slow cooker is different):
  - High—212°F–300°F
  - Low—170°F–200°F
  - Simmer—185°F
  - Warm—165°F

Cooked beans freeze well. Store them in freezer bags (squeeze the air out first) or freezer boxes. Cooked and dried bean measurements:
  - 16-oz. can, drained = about 1¾ cups beans
  - 19-oz. can, drained = about 2 cups beans
  - 1 lb. dried beans (about 2½ cups) = 5 cups cooked beans

Breakfasts

Apple Cinnamon Oatmeal

Hope Comerford, Clinton Township, MI

Makes 2–3 servings

Prep. Time: 5 minutes ⚜ *Cooking Time: 7 hours* ⚜ *Ideal slow-cooker size: 2-qt.*

½ cup steel cut oats

2 cups unsweetened vanilla almond milk

1 small apple, peeled and diced

¼ tsp. cinnamon

1. Spray crock with nonstick spray

2. Place all ingredients into crock and stir lightly.

3. Cover and cook on Low for 7 hours.

Serving suggestion:

Add a bit of sweetener of your choice if you wish at time of serving.

Calories: 172
Fat: 4g
Sodium: 124mg
Carbs: 29g
Sugar: 6g
Protein: 6g

Apple Oatmeal

Frances B. Musser, Newmanstown, PA

Makes 5 servings
Prep. Time: 20 minutes   ❧   Cooking Time: 3–5 hours   ❧   Ideal slow-cooker size: 3-qt.

2 cups fat-free milk
1 cup water
1 Tbsp. honey
1 Tbsp. coconut oil
¼ tsp. kosher salt
½ tsp. cinnamon
1 cup steel cut oats
1 cup chopped apples
½ cup chopped walnuts
1 Tbsp. turbinado sugar

1. Grease the inside of the slow-cooker crock.

2. Add all ingredients to crock and mix.

3. Cover. Cook on Low 3–5 hours.

Calories: 220
Fat: 12g
Sodium: 160mg
Carbs: 28.5g
Sugar: 14g
Protein: 8.5g

German Chocolate Oatmeal

Hope Comerford, Clinton Township, MI

Makes 4 servings
Prep. Time: 5 minutes & Cooking Time: 6–8 hours & Ideal slow-cooker size: 3-qt.

2 cups steel cut oats

8 cups unsweetened coconut milk

¼ cup unsweetened cocoa powder

¼ tsp. kosher salt

sweetened shredded coconut, to taste

1. Spray crock with nonstick spray.

2. Place steel cut oats, coconut milk, cocoa powder, and salt into crock and stir to mix.

3. Cover and cook on Low for 6–8 hours.

4. To serve, top each bowl of oatmeal with desired amount of shredded coconut.

Serving suggestion:

Sweeten with a bit of sweetener of your choice if you wish at time of serving.

Calories: 568

Fat: 11g

Sodium: 425mg

Carbs: 91g

Sugar: 33g

Protein: 13g

Oatmeal Morning

Barbara Forrester Landis, Lititz, PA

Makes 6 servings
Prep. Time: 10 minutes ⚜ *Cooking Time: 2½–6 hours* ⚜ *Ideal slow-cooker size: 3-qt.*

1 cup uncooked steel cut oats

1 cup dried cranberries

1 cup walnuts

½ tsp. kosher salt

1 Tbsp. cinnamon

2 cups water

2 cups fat-free nondairy milk (almond, rice, etc.)

1. Combine all dry ingredients in slow cooker. Stir well.

2. Add water and milk and stir.

3. Cover. Cook on High 2½ hours, or on Low 5–6 hours.

Calories: 260
Fat: 12g
Sodium: 215mg
Carbs: 38g
Sugar: 14g
Protein: 6g

Grain and Fruit Cereal

Cynthia Haller, New Holland, PA

Makes 4–5 servings

Prep. Time: 5 minutes ❧ *Cooking Time: 3½ hours* ❧ *Ideal slow-cooker size: 4-qt.*

⅓ cup uncooked quinoa

⅓ cup uncooked millet

⅓ cup uncooked brown rice

4 cups water

¼ tsp. salt

½ cup raisins or dried cranberries

¼ cup chopped nuts, *optional*

1 tsp. vanilla extract, *optional*

½ tsp. ground cinnamon, *optional*

1 Tbsp. maple syrup, *optional*

1. Wash the quinoa, millet, and brown rice and rinse well.

2. Place the grains, water, and salt in a slow cooker. Cook on Low until most of the water has been absorbed, about 3 hours.

3. Add dried fruit and any optional ingredients, and cook for 30 minutes more. If the mixture is too thick, add a little more water.

4. Serve hot or cold.

Serving suggestion:

Add a little nondairy milk to each bowl of cereal before serving.

Calories: 220
Fat: 2g
Sodium: 150mg
Carbs: 47g
Sugar: 11g
Protein: 5.5g

Warm 'n Fruity

Marlene Weaver, Lititz, PA

Makes 10 cups
Prep. Time: 10 minutes   &   Cooking Time: 6–7 hours   &   Ideal slow-cooker size: 5-qt.

5 cups water
2 cups seven-grain cereal
1 medium apple, peeled and chopped
1 cup unsweetened apple juice
¼ cup chopped dried apricots
¼ cup dried cranberries
¼ cup raisins
¼ cup chopped dates
¼ cup maple syrup
1 teaspoon cinnamon
½ teaspoon salt
chopped walnuts, *optional*

1. In the crock, combine all ingredients except for walnuts.

2. Cover and cook on Low for 6–7 hours or until fruits are softened.

3. Sprinkle individual servings with walnuts if desired.

Calories: 100
Fat: 0g
Sodium: 150mg
Carbs: 26.5g
Sugar: 16g
Protein: 1.5g

Granola

Hope Comerford, Clinton Township, MI

Makes about 10 cups
Prep. Time: 20 minutes   *&*   Cooking Time: 4–6 hours   *&*   Ideal slow-cooker size: 6- to 7-qt.

6 cups old-fashioned oats

¾ cup chopped almonds

½ cup chopped pecans

¾ cup raw sunflower seeds

¼ cup flaxseed

1 cup dried cranberries

1 cup chopped dehydrated apples

1 cup apple butter

¼ cup honey

¼ cup maple syrup

1. Place all of the dry ingredients in a bowl and stir.

2. Mix together the apple butter, honey, and maple syrup.

3. Spray your crock with nonstick spray.

4. Pour your granola mixture in the crock with the apple butter mixture on top. Mix thoroughly.

5. Cover and cook on Low with the lid vented for 4–6 hours, stirring frequently (every 30–40 minutes) or until the granola is lightly browned and slightly clumpy.

Calories: 293

Fat: 8g

Sodium: 12mg

Carbs: 50g

Sugar: 25g

Protein: 6g

Granola in the Slow Cooker

Earnie Zimmerman, Mechanicsburg, PA

Makes 10–12 servings
Prep. Time: 10 minutes   Cooking Time: 3–8 hours   Ideal slow-cooker size: 6-qt.

5 cups rolled oats

1 Tbsp. flaxseeds

¼ cup slivered almonds

¼ cup chopped pecans or walnuts

¼ cup unsweetened shredded coconut

¼ cup maple syrup or honey

¼ cup melted coconut oil

½ cup dried fruit

1. Spray slow-cooker crock with cooking spray. In slow cooker, mix together oats, flaxseeds, almonds, pecans or walnuts, and coconut.

2. Separately, combine maple syrup or honey and coconut oil. Pour over dry ingredients in cooker and toss well.

3. Place lid on slow cooker with a wooden spoon handle or chopstick venting one end of the lid.

4. Cook on High for 3–4 hours, stirring every 30 minutes, or cook on Low for 8 hours, stirring every hour. You may need to stir more often or cook for less time, depending on how hot your cooker cooks.

5. When granola smells good and toasty, pour it out onto a baking sheet to cool.

6. Add dried fruit to cooled granola and store in airtight container.

Calories: 260
Fat: 11.5g
Sodium: 5mg
Carbs: 35g
Sugar: 8g
Protein: 6g

Apple Granola

Phyllis Good, Lancaster, PA

Makes 12 servings

Prep. Time: 20 minutes ⚜ Cooking Time: 2–3 hours ⚜ Chilling Time: 1 hour ⚜ Ideal slow-cooker size: 5-qt.

9 cups unpeeled, sliced apples

1½ tsp. cinnamon

1½ cups dry rolled oats

1½ cups wheat germ

1½ cups whole wheat flour

1½ cups sunflower seeds

1⅓ cups water

¾ cup honey

1. Grease interior of slow-cooker crock.

2. Use your food processor to slice the apples. Place slices in slow cooker.

3. Sprinkle apple slices with cinnamon, and then stir together gently.

4. In a good-sized bowl, stir together dry rolled oats, wheat germ, whole wheat flour, and sunflower seeds.

5. When dry ingredients are well mixed, pour in water and honey. Using a sturdy spoon or your clean hands, mix thoroughly until wet ingredients are damp throughout.

6. Spoon over apples.

7. Cover, but vent the lid by propping it open with a chopstick or wooden spoon handle. Or if you're using an oval cooker, turn the lid sideways.

8. Cook on High for 1 hour, stirring up from the bottom and around the sides every 20 minutes or so. (Set a timer so you don't forget!)

9. Switch the cooker to Low. Bake another 1–2 hours, still stirring every 20 minutes or so.

10. Granola is done when it eventually browns a bit and looks dry.

11. Pour granola onto parchment or a large baking sheet to cool and crisp up more.

12. If you like clumps, no need to stir granola further while it cools. Otherwise, break up the granola with a spoon or your hands as it cools.

13. When completely cooled, store in airtight container.

Calories: 350
Fat: 11.5g
Sodium: 10mg
Carbs: 57.5g
Sugar: 26.5g
Protein: 10.5g

Apple Breakfast Cobbler

Anona M. Teel, Bangor, PA

Makes 8 servings

Prep. Time: 25 minutes ⚓ *Cooking Time: 2–9 hours* ⚓ *Ideal slow-cooker size: 4- or 5-qt.*

8 medium apples, cored, peeled, sliced

2 Tbsp. maple syrup

dash cinnamon

juice of 1 lemon

2 Tbsp. coconut oil, melted

2 cups homemade granola

1. Combine ingredients in slow cooker.

2. Cover. Cook on Low 7–9 hours (while you sleep!), or on High 2–3 hours (after you're up in the morning).

Calories: 210
Fat: 18.5g
Sodium: 20mg
Carbs: 61g
Sugar: 34g
Protein: 9.5g

Slow-Cooker Yogurt

Becky Fixel, Grosse Pointe Farms, MI

Makes 12–14 servings

Prep. Time: 2 minutes ❧ *Cooking Time: 12–14 hours* ❧ *Ideal slow-cooker size: 6-qt.*

I gallon whole milk

5.3-oz. container Greek yogurt with cultures

1. Empty the gallon of whole milk into your slow cooker and put it on High heat for 2–4 hours. Length of time depends on your model, but the milk needs to heat to just below boiling point, about 180–200°F.

2. Turn off your slow cooker and let your milk cool down to 110–115°F. Again, this will take 2–4 hours. Set your starter Greek yogurt out so it can reach room temperature during this step.

3. In a small bowl, add about 1 cup of the warm milk and the Greek yogurt and mix together. Pour the mixture into the milk in the slow cooker and mix it in by stirring back and forth. Replace the lid of your slow cooker and wrap the whole thing in a towel. Let sit for 12–14 hours, or, in other words, go to bed.

4. After 12 hours check on your glorious yogurt!

5. Line a colander with cheesecloth and place in bowl. Scoop your yogurt inside and let it sit for at least 4 hours. This will help separate the extra whey from the yogurt and thicken your final yogurt.

TIP

My yogurt didn't all fit in one colander, but thankfully I had a second one to use. You can wait until the yogurt sinks down and there is more space in the colander if you only have one. Spoon finished yogurt into jars or containers and place in the fridge. After your yogurt is done, you're going to have leftover whey. Put it in a jar and pop it in the fridge. Use it to replace stock in recipes, water your plants, or to make cheese. It's amazing what you can do with it!

Calories: 190

Fat: 10g

Sodium: 130mg

Carbs: 14.5g

Sugar: 15.5g

Protein: 10g

Chunky Applesauce

Colleen Heatwole, Burton, MI

Makes 8 servings
Prep. Time: 20 minutes ⚘ *Cooking Time: 8–10 hours* ⚘ *Ideal slow-cooker size: 5-qt.*

10 large cooking apples such as Granny Smith, Fuji, Braeburn, Jonagold, or Cameo

½ cup water

1 tsp. ground cinnamon

¼ cup turbinado sugar

1. Peel, core, and chop apples.

2. Combine apples with rest of ingredients in slow cooker.

3. Cover and cook on Low for 8–10 hours. Serve warm.

Calories: 133
Fat: 0.5g
Sodium: 3mg
Carbs: 36g
Sugar: 27g
Protein: 0g

French Toast Casserole

Michele Ruvola, Vestal, NY

Makes 9 servings

Prep. Time: 30 minutes ❧ *Cooking Time: 2–4 hours* ❧ *Ideal slow-cooker size: 5- to 6½-qt.*

2 eggs

2 egg whites

1 ½ cups milk nonfat milk

5 Tbsp. honey, *divided*

1 tsp. vanilla extract

2 tsp. cinnamon, *divided*

3 cups finely diced apple

⅓ cup chopped, toasted pecans

1 tsp. lemon juice

9 slices whole-grain bread

1. In a mixing bowl, whisk together eggs, egg whites, milk, 2 Tbsp. honey, vanilla, and 1 tsp. cinnamon.

2. Separately, combine remaining 3 Tbsp. honey, remaining 1 tsp. cinnamon, apple, pecans, and lemon juice. Set aside.

3. In a greased slow cooker, place one layer of bread, cutting to fit (triangles are good).

4. Layer in ¼ of the apple filling. Repeat layers, making 3 layers of bread and 4 of filling, ending with filling on top.

5. Pour egg mixture gently over everything.

6. Cover and cook on High 2–2½ hours or on Low 4 hours, or until bread has soaked up the liquid and apples are soft.

Serving suggestion:
Serve with warm maple syrup if desired.

Calories: 199

Fat: 5g

Sodium: 145mg

Carbs: 33g

Sugar: 20g

Protein: 8g

Italian Frittata

Hope Comerford, Clinton Township, MI

Makes 6 servings
Prep. Time: 10 minutes   ⚶   Cooking Time: 3–4 hours   ⚶   Ideal slow-cooker size: 5- or 6-qt.

10 eggs
1 Tbsp. chopped fresh basil
1 Tbsp. chopped fresh mint
1 Tbsp. chopped fresh sage
1 Tbsp. chopped fresh oregano
½ tsp. sea salt
1/8 tsp. pepper
1 Tbsp. grated Parmesan cheese
¼ cup diced prosciutto
½ cup chopped onion

1. Spray your crock with nonstick spray.

2. In a bowl, mix together the eggs, basil, mint, sage, oregano, sea salt, pepper, and Parmesan. Pour this mixture into the crock.

3. Sprinkle the prosciutto and onion evenly over the egg mixture in the crock.

4. Cover and cook on Low for 3–4 hours.

Calories: 145
Fat: 9g
Sodium: 370mg
Carbs: 2.5g
Sugar: 1g
Protein: 12.5g

Fresh Veggie and Herb Omelet

Hope Comerford, Clinton Township, MI

Makes 8 servings
Prep. Time: 20 minutes & Cooking Time: 4½–6½ hours & Ideal slow-cooker size: 6-qt.

12 eggs

1 cup unsweetened almond milk

½ tsp. kosher salt

¼ tsp. pepper

3 cloves garlic, minced

1 tsp. fresh chopped basil

6 dashes hot sauce

2 cups broccoli florets

1 yellow bell pepper, diced

1 red bell pepper, diced

1 onion, diced

1 cup crumbled feta cheese

1 cup diced cherry tomatoes

½ cup fresh chopped parsley

1. Spray crock with nonstick spray.

2. In a bowl, mix together eggs, milk, salt, pepper, garlic, basil, and hot sauce.

3. Place broccoli, yellow pepper, red pepper, and onion in crock. Gently mix with a spoon.

4. Pour egg mixture over the top.

5. Cover and cook on Low for 4–6 hours, or until center is set.

6. Sprinkle feta over the top, then cook an additional 30 minutes.

7. To serve, sprinkle the omelet with the chopped tomatoes and fresh parsley.

Calories: 188
Fat: 12g
Sodium: 449mg
Carbs: 7g
Sugar: 3g
Protein: 13g

Turkey Bacon, Spinach, and Gruyère Quiche

Hope Comerford, Clinton Township, MI

Makes 4–6 servings
Prep. Time: 15 minutes ⚜ *Cooking Time: 3–4 hours* ⚜ *Ideal slow-cooker size: 6-qt.*

8 eggs

1 cup unsweetened almond milk

1 tsp. salt

1 tsp. pepper

1 tsp. garlic powder

1 tsp. onion powder

½ cup chopped onion

5 slices turkey bacon, diced

2 handfuls (about 2 oz.) fresh spinach leaves

8 oz. Gruyère cheese, shredded

1. In a bowl, mix together the eggs, milk, salt, pepper, garlic powder, and onion powder. Pour this into the bottom of your greased crock.

2. Sprinkle the onion and bacon evenly over the surface of the eggs.

3. Spread the spinach all over the top of the egg mixture in your crock.

4. Cover the spinach with the shredded cheese.

5. Cover and cook on Low for 3–4 hours, or until it is completely set in the middle.

Calories: 305
Fat: 22g
Sodium: 940mg
Carbs: 4g
Sugar: 1g
Protein: 24g

Crustless Spinach Quiche

Barbara Hoover, Landisville, PA

Makes 8 servings
Prep. Time: 15 minutes ☙ *Cooking Time: 2–4 hours* ☙ *Ideal slow-cooker size: 3- or 4-qt.*

2 10-oz. pkgs. frozen chopped spinach

2 cups cottage cheese

¼ cup coconut oil

1½ cups cubed sharp cheddar cheese

3 eggs, beaten

¼ cup all-purpose gluten-free flour

1 tsp. salt

1. Grease interior of slow-cooker crock.

2. Thaw spinach completely. Squeeze as dry as you can. Then place in crock.

3. Stir in all other ingredients and combine well.

4. Cover. Cook on Low 2–4 hours, or until quiche is set. Stick blade of knife into center of quiche. If blade comes out clean, quiche is set. If it doesn't, cover and cook another 15 minutes or so.

5. When cooked, allow to stand 10–15 minutes so mixture can firm up. Then serve.

Calories: 250
Fat: 18.5g
Sodium: 675mg
Carbs: 7.5g
Sugar: 2.5g
Protein: 15.5g

Huevos Rancheros in Crock

Pat Bishop, Bedminster, PA

Makes 6 servings

Prep. Time: 25 minutes ❧ *Cooking Time: 2 hours* ❧ *Ideal slow-cooker size: 6-qt.*

3 cups gluten-free salsa, room temperature

2 cups cooked beans, drained, room temperature

6 eggs, room temperature

salt and pepper, to taste

⅓ cup grated Mexican-blend cheese, *optional*

6 white corn tortillas, for serving

1. Mix salsa and beans in slow cooker.

2. Cook on High for 1 hour or until steaming.

3. With a spoon, make 6 evenly spaced dents in the salsa mixture; try not to expose the bottom of the crock. Break an egg into each dent.

4. Salt and pepper eggs. Sprinkle with cheese if you wish.

5. Cover and continue to cook on High until egg whites are set and yolks are as firm as you like them, approximately 20–40 minutes.

6. To serve, scoop out an egg with some beans and salsa. Serve with warm tortillas.

Calories: 200
Fat: 1g
Sodium: 975mg
Carbs: 36g
Sugar: 6g
Protein: 12g

Breakfast Polenta

Margaret W. High, Lancaster, PA

Makes 8–10 servings
Prep. Time: 20 minutes & Cooking Time: 2½ hours & Ideal slow-cooker size: 5- or 6-qt.

4 eggs, room temperature

2 cups nonfat milk, room temperature

2 cups stone-ground (coarse) cornmeal

2/3 cup shredded Parmesan cheese, *divided*

4 cups boiling water

2 Tbsp. finely diced onion

2 cups chopped fresh spinach

1 tsp. kosher salt

pepper, to taste

1. In a large mixing bowl, beat eggs. Whisk in milk, cornmeal, and ⅓ cup Parmesan.

2. Whisk in boiling water.

3. Gently stir in onion, spinach, salt, and pepper.

4. Pour mixture into well-greased slow cooker.

5. Cover and cook on High for 2 hours, stirring once to be sure cornmeal is evenly distributed as it cooks.

6. When polenta is thick, sprinkle with remaining ⅓ cup Parmesan. Remove lid and allow to cook on High for an additional 30 minutes as cheese melts and any extra liquid evaporates. Polenta will be softer when hot, but will firm up as it cools. Serve hot, warm, or chilled.

Calories: 157
Fat: 4g
Sodium: 346mg
Carbs: 22g
Sugar: 3g
Protein: 8g

Fiesta Hash Browns

Dena Mell-Dorchy, Royal Oak, MI

Makes 8 servings
Prep. Time: 15 minutes & Cooking Time: 8–9 hours & Ideal slow-cooker size: 3- or 4-qt.

1 lb. ground turkey sausage
½ cup chopped onion
5 cups frozen diced hash browns
8 oz. low sodium chicken stock
1 small red sweet pepper
1 jalapeño, seeded and finely diced
1 ½ cups sliced mushrooms
2 Tbsp. quick-cooking tapioca
½ cup shredded Monterey Jack cheese

1. Spray slow cooker with nonstick spray.

2. In a large skillet, brown sausage and onion over medium heat. Drain off fat.

3. Combine sausage mixture, hash browns, chicken stock, sweet pepper, jalapeño, mushrooms, and quick-cooking tapioca in cooker; stir to combine.

4. Cover and cook on Low heat for 8–9 hours. Stir before serving. Top with shredded Monterey Jack cheese.

Calories: 275
Fat: 10g
Sodium: 500mg
Carbs: 29g
Sugar: 2g
Protein: 18g

Italian Sausage and Sweet Pepper Hash

Hope Comerford, Clinton Township, MI

Makes 6–8 servings
Prep. Time: 10 minutes & Cooking Time: 6½ hours & Ideal slow-cooker size: 4-qt.

12-oz. pkg. Italian turkey sausage, cut lengthwise, then into ½-inch pieces

16 oz. frozen diced potatoes

1½ cups sliced sweet onion

1 yellow pepper, sliced

1 green pepper, sliced

1 red pepper, sliced

¼ cup melted butter

1 tsp. sea salt

½ tsp. pepper

½ tsp. dried thyme

½ tsp. dried parsley

½ cup shredded reduced-fat Swiss cheese

1. Spray crock with nonstick spray.

2. Place sausage, frozen potatoes, onion, and sliced peppers into crock.

3. Mix melted butter with salt, pepper, thyme, and parsley. Pour over contents of crock and stir.

4. Cover and cook on Low for 6 hours. Sprinkle with the Swiss cheese, then cover and cook for an additional 20 minutes, or until the cheese is melted.

Calories: 218
Fat: 16g
Sodium: 619mg
Carbs: 5g
Sugar: 2g
Protein: 14g

Soups, Stews, and Chilies

SOUPS

Steak and Wild Rice Soup

Sally Holzem, Schofield, WI

Makes 6 servings

Prep. Time: 15 minutes ☙ *Cooking Time: 5 hours* ☙ *Ideal slow-cooker size: 5-qt.*

4 cups beef stock

3 cups cubed, cooked roast beef

4 oz. fresh mushrooms, sliced

½ cup chopped onion

¼ cup ketchup

2 tsp. apple cider vinegar

1 tsp. brown sugar

1 tsp. gluten-free Worcestershire sauce

⅛ tsp. ground mustard

1½ cups cooked wild rice

1 cup frozen peas

1. Combine stock, beef, mushrooms, onion, ketchup, vinegar, sugar, Worcestershire sauce, and mustard in slow cooker.

2. Cook on Low 4 hours.

3. Add rice and peas. Cook an additional hour on Low.

TIP

Great way to use up scraps of meat and broth left from a roast beef, and a nice way to transform leftover wild rice.

Calories: 142
Fat: 2g
Sodium: 460mg
Carbs: 20g
Sugar: 6g
Protein: 13g

Beef Barley Soup

Michelle Showalter, Bridgewater, VA

Makes 10–12 servings
Prep. Time: 15 minutes ❧ Cooking Time: 4–10 hours ❧ Ideal slow-cooker size: 6-qt.

1 lb. extra-lean ground beef

1½ qts. water

1 qt. canned tomatoes, stewed, crushed, or whole

3 cups sliced carrots

1 cup diced celery

1 cup diced potatoes

1 cup diced onions

¾ cup quick-cooking barley

3 tsp. low-sodium beef bouillon granules, or 3 low-sodium beef bouillon cubes

2 tsp. kosher salt

¼ tsp. pepper

1. Brown ground beef in skillet. Stir frequently to break up clumps of meat. When meat is no longer pink, drain off drippings.

2. Place meat in cooker, along with all other ingredients. Mix together well.

3. Cover. Cook on Low 8–10 hours or on High 4–5 hours.

Variation:

You may use pearl barley instead of quick-cooking barley. Cook it in a saucepan according to package directions, and add halfway through soup's cooking time.

Calories: 139
Fat: 3g
Sodium: 500mg
Carbs: 17g
Sugar: 498g
Protein: 11g

Cabbage and Beef Soup

Colleen Heatwole, Burton, MI

Makes 6–8 servings
Prep. Time: 20 minutes ⚜ *Cooking Time: 6–8 hours* ⚜ *Ideal slow-cooker size: 6-qt.*

1 lb. extra-lean ground beef

28- or 32-oz. can tomatoes or 1 qt. home-canned tomatoes

¼ tsp. onion powder

1 tsp. garlic powder

¼ tsp. pepper

16-oz. can kidney beans, drained and rinsed

2 stalks celery, chopped

½ head cabbage, chopped

8 cups low-sodium beef stock

¼ cup water

chopped fresh parsley, for garnish

1. Brown beef in large skillet, then drain any drippings. Add tomatoes and chop coarsely. Transfer to slow cooker.

2. Add remaining ingredients except parsley.

3. Cover and cook 6–8 hours on Low.

4. Serve in bowls garnished with fresh parsley.

TIP

Lean ground turkey may be used. Black beans or small red beans may be substituted for the kidney beans. This soup freezes well.

Calories: 214
Fat: 5g
Sodium: 636mg
Carbs: 20g
Sugar: 5g
Protein: 23g

The Best Bean and Ham Soup

Hope Comerford, Clinton Township, MI

Makes 8–10 servings

Prep. Time: 8 minutes ❧ *Soaking Time: 8 hours or overnight* ❧ *Cooking Time: 8–12 hours*
Ideal slow-cooker size: 7-qt.

1 meaty ham bone or shank
1 lb. dry navy beans
1 cup chopped onions
2 cloves garlic, minced
1 cup chopped celery
¼ cup chopped parsley
1 Tbsp. sea salt
1 tsp. pepper
1 tsp. nutmeg
1 tsp. oregano
1 tsp. basil
2 bay leaves
8 cups low-sodium chicken stock
6–8 cups water

1. Place the ham bone in the bottom of the crock and pour all of the remaining ingredients into the crock around it, ending with the water. You'll want to make sure you've covered the ham bone with water.

2. Cover and cook on Low for 8–12 hours.

Calories: 266
Fat: 4g
Sodium: 1032mg
Carbs: 37g
Sugar: 6g
Protein: 20g

Navy Bean and Ham Soup

Jennifer Freed, Rockingham, VA

Makes 6 servings
Prep. Time: overnight, or approximately 8 hours ½ Cooking Time: 8–10 hours ½ Ideal slow-cooker size: 6½- or 7-qt.

6 cups water

5 cups dried navy beans, soaked overnight, drained, and rinsed

1 pound ham, cubed

15-oz. can corn, drained

4-oz. can mild diced green chilies, drained

1 onion, diced, *optional*

salt and pepper, to taste

1. Place all ingredients in slow cooker.

2. Cover and cook on Low 8–10 hours, or until beans are tender.

Calories: 420
Fat: 5g
Sodium: 1200mg
Carbs: 103g
Sugar: 7g
Protein: 44g

Black Bean and Ham Soup

Colleen Heatwole, Burton, MI

Makes 4 servings
Prep. Time: 30 minutes ❧ Cooking Time: 6–8 hours ❧ Ideal slow-cooker size: 5-qt.

2 cups chopped carrots

1 cup chopped celery

2 cloves garlic, minced

1 medium onion, chopped

2 15½-oz. cans black beans, undrained

3½ cups low-sodium chicken or vegetable broth

15-oz. can crushed tomatoes

1½ tsp. dried basil

½ tsp. dried oregano

½ tsp. ground cumin

½ tsp. chili powder

¼ tsp. hot pepper sauce

1 cup diced cooked ham

1. Combine all ingredients in slow cooker.

2. Cover and cook on Low 6–8 hours or until vegetables are tender.

Calories: 379
Fat: 6g
Sodium: 1264mg
Carbs: 53g
Sugar: 13g
Protein: 24g

Ham and Beans

Jenny R. Unternahrer, Wayland, IA

Makes 6–8 servings
Prep. Time: 10 minutes ♣ Cooking Time: 6–8 hours ♣ Ideal slow-cooker size: 6-qt.

1-lb. bag dried great northern beans

Leftover ham chunks (approx. 1–2 lbs.)

6 cups water, or low-sodium chicken or vegetable broth

1½ Tbsp. minced garlic

1 medium onion, chopped

½ tsp. salt

1. Sort through your beans to make sure there aren't any rocks (yes, sometimes they make it through processing) or any odd-looking beans. Rinse. Place beans and rest of the ingredients in the slow cooker.

2. Cover and cook on Low for 6–8 hours, or until beans are tender.

3. Shred the ham a little so everyone gets both beans and ham in their bowl.

Serving suggestion:

Great served with a slice of cornbread.

TIP
This recipe does great doubled. Just cook for approximately 12 hours on Low.

Calories: 293
Fat: 5g
Sodium: 683mg
Carbs: 37g
Sugar: 2g
Protein: 25g

Grandma's Barley Soup

Andrea O'Neil, Fairfield, CT

Makes 10–12 servings
Prep. Time: 10 minutes & Cooking Time: 6–8 hours & Ideal slow-cooker size: 4- or 5-qt.

2 smoked ham hocks
4 carrots, sliced
4 potatoes, cubed
1 cup dry lima beans
1 cup low-sodium tomato paste
1½–2 cups cooked barley
water
salt, if needed

1. Combine all ingredients in slow cooker, except salt.

2. Cover with water.

3. Cover. Simmer on Low 6–8 hours, or until both ham and beans are tender.

4. Debone ham hocks and return cut-up meat to soup.

5. Taste before serving. Add salt if needed.

TIP
If you want to reduce the amount of meat you eat, this dish is flavorful using only 1 ham hock.

Calories: 221
Fat: 6g
Sodium: 298mg
Carbs: 28g
Sugar: 6g
Protein: 15g

Shredded Pork Tortilla Soup

Hope Comerford, Clinton Township, MI

Makes 6–8 servings
Prep. Time: 10 minutes   Cooking Time: 8–10 hours   Ideal slow-cooker size: 5-qt.

3 large tomatoes, chopped
1 cup chopped red onion
1 jalapeño, seeded and minced
1-lb. pork loin
2 tsp. cumin
2 tsp. chili powder
2 tsp. onion powder
2 tsp. garlic powder
2 tsp. lime juice
8 cups low-sodium chicken stock

garnish, *optional:*
fresh chopped cilantro
tortilla chips
avocado slices
freshly grated Mexican cheese

1. In your crock, place the tomatoes, onion, and jalapeño.

2. Place the pork loin on top.

3. Add all the seasonings and lime juice, then pour in the chicken stock.

4. Cover and cook on Low for 8–10 hours.

5. Remove the pork and shred it between two forks. Place it back into the soup and stir.

6. Serve each bowl of soup with fresh chopped cilantro, tortilla chips, avocado slices, and freshly grated Mexican cheese, if desired . . . or any other garnishes you would like!

TIP
If you don't have time for freshly chopped tomatoes, use a can of diced or chopped tomatoes.

Calories: 226
Fat: 8g
Sodium: 398mg
Carbs: 14g
Sugar: 6g
Protein: 23g

Chicken Noodle Soup

Jennifer J. Gehman, Harrisburg, PA

Makes 6–8 servings
Prep. Time: 5–10 minutes   ⚜   Cooking Time: 4–8 hours   ⚜   Ideal slow-cooker size: 5-qt.

2 cups uncooked cubed chicken, dark or white meat

15¼-oz. can corn, or 2 cups frozen corn

1 cup green beans, or peas*

10 cups low-sodium chicken broth

½ pkg. dry kluski (or other very sturdy) noodles

1. Combine all ingredients except noodles in slow cooker.

2. Cover. Cook on High 4–6 hours or on Low 6–8 hours.

3. Two hours before end of cooking time, stir in noodles.

*If using green beans, stir in during Step 1. If using peas, stir into slow cooker just 20 minutes before end of cooking time.

Serving Suggestion:
Garnish with microgreens or parsley and fresh cracked pepper.

Calories: 188
Fat: 3g
Sodium: 947mg
Carbs: 23g
Sugar: 2g
Protein: 18g

Chicken and Vegetable Soup

Hope Comerford, Clinton Township, MI

Makes 4–6 servings
Prep. Time: 15 minutes ❧ Cooking Time: 7–8 hours ❧ Ideal slow-cooker size: 5-qt.

1 lb. boneless skinless chicken, cut into bite-sized pieces

2 stalks celery, diced

1 small yellow squash, diced

4 oz. mushrooms, sliced

2 large carrots, diced

1 medium onion, chopped

2 Tbsp. garlic powder

1 Tbsp. onion powder

1 Tbsp. basil

½ tsp. no-salt seasoning

1 tsp. salt

black pepper, to taste

32 oz. low-sodium chicken stock

1. Place the chicken, vegetables, and spices into the crock. Pour the chicken stock over the top.

2. Cover and cook on Low for 7–8 hours, or until vegetables are tender.

Calories: 160
Fat: 2g
Sodium: 700mg
Carbs: 13g
Sugar: 5g
Protein: 23g

Chicken and Vegetable Soup with Rice

Hope Comerford, Clinton Township, MI

Makes 6–8 servings
Prep. Time: 20 minutes ⚬ Cooking Time: 6½–7½ hours ⚬ Ideal slow-cooker size: 3-qt.

1½–2 lbs. boneless, skinless chicken breasts

1½ cups chopped carrots

1½ cups chopped red onion

2 Tbsp. garlic powder

1 Tbsp. onion powder

2 tsp. kosher salt (you can omit the salt if you're using regular stock rather than no-salt)

¼ tsp. celery seed

¼ tsp. paprika

⅛ tsp. pepper

1 dried bay leaf

8 cups no-salt chicken stock

1 cup fresh green beans

3 cups cooked rice

1. Place chicken into the bottom of crock, then add rest of the remaining ingredients, except green beans and rice.

2. Cover and cook on Low for 6–7 hours.

3. Remove chicken and chop into bite-sized cubes. Place chicken back into crock and add in green beans. Cover and cook another 30 minutes.

4. To serve, place approximately ½ cup of the cooked rice into each bowl and ladle soup over top of the rice.

Calories: 332
Fat: 6g
Sodium: 894mg
Carbs: 32g
Sugar: 7g
Protein: 35g

Chicken Tortilla Soup

Becky Fixel, Grosse Pointe Farms, MI

Makes 10–12 servings
Prep. Time: 5 minutes ❧ Cooking Time: 7–8 hours ❧ Ideal slow-cooker size: 5-qt.

2 lbs. boneless skinless chicken breast
32 oz. chicken stock
14 oz. salsa verde
10-oz. can diced tomatoes with lime juice
15-oz. can sweet corn, drained
1 Tbsp. minced garlic
1 small onion, diced
1 Tbsp. chili pepper
½ tsp. fresh ground pepper
½ tsp. salt
½ tsp. oregano
1 Tbsp. dried jalapeño slices

1. Add all ingredients to your slow cooker.

2. Cook on Low for 7–8 hours.

3. Approximately 30 minutes before the end, remove your chicken and shred it into small pieces.

Serving suggestion:
Top with a dollop of nonfat plain Greek yogurt, shredded cheese, fresh jalapeños, or fresh cilantro.

Calories: 150
Fat: 3g
Sodium: 630mg
Carbs: 9g
Sugar: 4g
Protein: 20g

Chicken Tortilla Soup

Amy Troyer, Garden Grove, IA

Makes 8 cups
Prep. Time: 30 minutes ❧ Cooking Time: 3 hours ❧ Ideal slow-cooker size: 4-qt.

2 Tbsp. olive oil

¾ cup chopped onion

¼ cup chopped carrots

¼ cup chopped celery

¼ cup chopped sweet pepper (green or red)

1 clove garlic, minced

½ tsp. chili powder

½ tsp. paprika

½ tsp. dried oregano

1 tsp. cumin

1 tsp. coriander, *optional*

dash red pepper

1½ cups cooked shredded chicken

1 qt. low-sodium chicken broth

1 cup water

½ cup fresh chunked tomatoes

1½ tsp. salt

½ tsp. pepper

½ cup cream

1 cup shredded cheddar cheese

Crushed tortilla chips, for serving

1. Heat oil in a saucepan and sauté onion, carrots, celery, and peppers.

2. Add the garlic and spices and fry together for 1–2 minutes.

3. In slow cooker, place the sautéed vegetables, chicken, chicken broth, water, tomatoes, salt, and pepper.

4. Cover and cook for 3 hours on Low.

5. Add cream and cheese. Stir until cheese is melted.

6. Serve with crushed tortilla chips.

Serving suggestion:
If you would like to make this soup more of a hearty main-dish soup, add ¾ cup frozen corn and 1 can white kidney beans, drained, toward the end of cooking time (just long enough to cook the corn and warm the beans).

Calories: 107
Fat: 8g
Sodium: 310mg
Carbs: 2g
Sugar: 1g
Protein: 8g

Chicken Chickpea Tortilla Soup

Hope Comerford, Clinton Township, MI

Makes 4–6 servings
Prep. Time: 5 minutes & Cooking Time: 6 hours & Ideal slow-cooker size: 4-qt.

2 boneless skinless chicken breasts

2 14½-oz. cans petite diced tomatoes

15-oz. can garbanzo beans (chickpeas), drained

6 cups chicken stock

1 onion, chopped

4-oz. can diced green chilies

1 tsp. cilantro

3–4 cloves garlic, minced

1 tsp. sea salt

1 tsp. pepper

1 tsp. cumin

1 tsp. paprika

1. Place all ingredients in slow cooker.

2. Cover and cook on Low for 6 hours.

3. Use two forks to pull chicken into shreds.

Serving suggestion:
Serve with a small dollop of nonfat Greek yogurt, a little shredded cheddar, and some baked blue corn tortilla chips.

Calories: 420
Fat: 9g
Sodium: 1400mg
Carbs: 48.5g
Sugar: 18.5g
Protein: 38.5g

Southwest Chicken and White Bean Soup

Karen Ceneviva, Seymour, CT

Makes 6 servings
Prep. Time: 15 minutes & Cooking Time: 4–10 hours & Ideal slow-cooker size: 3½-qt.

I lb. boneless, skinless chicken breasts, cut into 1-inch cubes

1¾ cups low-sodium chicken broth

I cup chunky salsa

3 cloves garlic, minced

2 Tbsp. cumin

15½-oz. can small white beans, drained and rinsed

I cup frozen corn

I large onion, chopped

1. Add all ingredients to the slow cooker. Stir well.

2. Cover. Cook 8–10 hours on Low or 4–5 hours on High.

Calories: 260
Fat: 3g
Sodium: 566mg
Carbs: 30g
Sugar: 5g
Protein: 28g

Taco Bean Soup

Colleen Heatwole, Burton, MI

Makes 8–10 servings
Prep. Time: 20 minutes ❧ Cooking Time: 4–6 hours ❧ Ideal slow-cooker size: 6-qt.

1 lb. lean ground turkey

1 large onion, chopped

14-oz. can pinto beans, undrained

15-oz. can black beans, undrained

15-oz. can kidney beans, undrained

2 14½-oz. cans peeled and diced tomatoes or 1 qt. fresh tomatoes

15-oz. can low-sodium tomato sauce

4-oz. can diced green chilies

1 pkg. low-sodium taco seasoning

15-oz. can whole-kernel corn, undrained

1. Brown ground turkey and onion in skillet.

2. Place turkey mixture in slow cooker along with other ingredients.

3. Cook on Low 4–6 hours.

Serving suggestion:

Serve with sour cream, grated cheese, and tortilla chips.

TIP
Any beans can be used in this recipe. You can keep frozen beans that you have cooked on hand and just use a combination.

Calories: 297
Fat: 1.5g
Sodium: 223mg
Carbs: 49g
Sugar: 7g
Protein: 25g

Turkey Frame Soup

Joyce Zuercher, Hesston, KS

Makes 6–8 servings
Prep. Time: 40 minutes & Cooking Time: 3–4 hours & Ideal slow-cooker size: 6-qt.

2–3 cups cooked and cut-up turkey*

3 qts. turkey or chicken broth

1 onion, diced

½–¾ tsp. salt, or to taste

16-oz. can diced tomatoes

1 Tbsp. low-sodium chicken bouillon granules

1 tsp. dried thyme

1/8 tsp. pepper

1½ tsp. dried oregano

4 cups chopped fresh vegetables—any combination of sliced celery, carrots, onions, rutabaga, broccoli, cauliflower, mushrooms, and more

1½ cups uncooked gluten-free noodles

*If you've got a big turkey frame, and you know it's got some good meaty morsels on it, here's what to do: Break it up enough to fit into your Dutch oven. Add 3 qts. water, 1 onion, quartered, and 2 tsp. salt. Cover, and simmer 1½ hours. Remove turkey bones from Dutch oven and allow to cool. Then debone and chop meat coarsely. Discard bones and skin. Strain broth. Begin with Step 1 above!

1. Place turkey, broth, onion, salt, tomatoes, bouillon granules, thyme, pepper, oregano, and vegetables into slow cooker. Stir.

2. Cover. Cook on Low 3–4 hours, or until vegetables are nearly done.

3. Fifteen to 30 minutes before serving time, stir in noodles. Cover. Cook on Low. If noodles are thin and small, they'll cook in 15 minutes or less. If heavier, they may need 30 minutes to become tender.

4. Stir well before serving.

Calories: 166
Fat: 2g
Sodium: 2043mg
Carbs: 13g
Sugar: 5g
Protein: 19g

Turkey Meatball Soup

Mary Ann Lefever, Lancaster, PA

Makes 8 servings
Prep. Time: 30 minutes ❧ Cooking Time: 8 hours ❧ Ideal slow-cooker size: 5- or 6-qt.

4–5 large carrots, chopped

10 cups low-sodium chicken broth

¾ lb. escarole, washed and cut into bite-sized pieces

1 lb. lean ground turkey, uncooked

1 medium onion, chopped

2 large eggs, beaten

½ cup bread crumbs

½ cup freshly grated Parmesan, plus more for serving

1 tsp. salt

¼ tsp. pepper

1. In slow cooker, combine carrots and broth.

2. Stir in escarole.

3. Cover. Cook on Low 4 hours.

4. Combine turkey, onion, eggs, bread crumbs, ½ cup Parmesan cheese, salt, and pepper in good-sized bowl. Mix well and shape into 1-inch balls. Drop carefully into soup.

5. Cover cooker. Cook on Low 4 more hours, or just until meatballs and vegetables are cooked through.

6. Serve hot sprinkled with extra Parmesan cheese.

Variation:

If you wish, you can substitute 3 cups cut-up cooked turkey for the ground turkey meatballs.

Calories: 199
Fat: 5g
Sodium: 1401mg
Carbs: 12g
Sugar: 3g
Protein: 24g

Kielbasa Soup

Bernice M. Gnidovec, Streator, IL

Makes 8 servings
Prep. Time: 10 minutes   ♣   Cooking Time: 12 hours   ♣   Ideal slow-cooker size: 8-qt.

16-oz. pkg. frozen mixed vegetables, or your choice of vegetables

6-oz. can tomato paste

1 medium onion, chopped

3 medium potatoes, diced

1½ lbs. turkey kielbasa, cut into ¼-inch pieces

4 qts. water

1. Combine all ingredients in large slow cooker.
2. Cover. Cook on Low 12 hours.

Calories: 230
Fat: 9g
Sodium: 1226mg
Carbs: 23g
Sugar: 7g
Protein: 15g

Slow-Cooker Tomato Soup

Becky Fixel, Grosse Pointe Farms, MI

Makes 8 servings
Prep. Time: 15 minutes ❧ *Cooking Time: 6 hours* ❧ *Ideal slow-cooker size: 6-qt.*

6–8 cups chopped fresh tomatoes

1 medium onion, chopped

2 tsp. minced garlic

1 tsp. basil

½ tsp. pepper

½ tsp. sea salt

½ tsp. red pepper flakes

2 Tbsp. chicken bouillon

1 cup water

¾ cup fat-free half-and-half

1. Combine your tomatoes, onion, spices, chicken bouillon, and 1 cup of water in your slow cooker.

2. Cover and cook on Low for 6 hours.

3. Add in your ¾ cup fat-free half-and-half and combine all ingredients with an immersion blender. Serve hot.

Calories: 70
Fat: 0g
Sodium: 470mg
Carbs: 11g
Sugar: 6g
Protein: 1g

Fresh Tomato Soup

Rebecca Plank Leichty, Harrisonburg, VA

Makes 6 servings

Prep. Time: 20–25 minutes ♣ Cooking Time: 3–4 hours ♣ Ideal slow-cooker size: 3½- to 4-qt.

5 cups diced ripe tomatoes (your choice about whether or not to peel them)

1 Tbsp. tomato paste

4 cups chicken or vegetable broth

1 carrot, grated

1 onion, minced

1 Tbsp. minced garlic

1 tsp. dried basil

Pepper, to taste

2 Tbsp. lemon juice

1 dried bay leaf

1. Combine all ingredients in a slow cooker.

2. Cook on Low for 3–4 hours. Stir once while cooking.

3. Remove bay leaf before serving.

Calories: 69
Fat: 10g
Sodium: 534mg
Carbs: 10g
Sugar: 6g
Protein: 5g

Creamy Tomato Soup

Susie Shenk Wenger, Lancaster, PA

Makes 4 servings
Prep. Time: 10–15 minutes   Cooking Time: 3–4 hours   Ideal slow-cooker size: 3-qt.

29-oz. can tomato sauce, or crushed tomatoes, or I qt. home-canned tomatoes, chopped

I small onion, chopped

1–2 carrots, sliced thinly

I tsp. brown sugar

I tsp. Italian seasoning

¼ tsp. sea salt

¼ tsp. pepper

I tsp. freshly chopped parsley

½ tsp. gluten-free Worcestershire sauce

I cup heavy whipping cream

croutons, preferably homemade, *optional*

freshly grated Parmesan cheese, *optional*

1. Combine tomato sauce, onion, carrots, brown sugar, Italian seasoning, salt, pepper, parsley, and Worcestershire sauce in slow cooker.

2. Cover. Cook on Low 3–4 hours, or until vegetables are soft.

3. Cool soup a bit. Puree with immersion blender.

4. Add cream and blend lightly again.

5. Serve hot with croutons and Parmesan as garnish.

TIP
This recipe can easily be doubled.

Calories: 274
Fat: 22g
Sodium: 1106mg
Carbs: 17g
Sugar: 12g
Protein: 5g

French Onion Soup

Hope Comerford, Clinton Township, MI

Makes 6–8 servings
Prep. Time: 10 minutes ❧ Cooking Time: 7–8 hours ❧ Ideal slow-cooker size: 5-qt.

3–4 large sweet yellow onions, sliced thinly

½ tsp. pepper

1 bay leaf

2 sprigs fresh thyme

7 cups low-sodium beef stock

1 cup dry white wine (such as a chardonnay)

6–8 slices bread, crusts removed

4 oz. Gruyère cheese, sliced thinly

1. Place all of the onions into the crock and sprinkle them with the pepper. Add the bay leaf and sprigs of thyme.

2. Pour in the beef stock and wine.

3. Cover and cook on Low for 7–8 hours. Remove the thyme sprigs and bay leaf.

4. Serve each serving of soup in an oven-safe bowl and cover the soup with a slice of bread topped with cheese. Place it in the oven under the broiler for a few minutes, or until the cheese starts to bubble.

Calories: 178
Fat: 5g
Sodium: 626mg
Carbs: 17g
Sugar: 5g
Protein: 10g

Vegetarian Split Pea Soup

Colleen Heatwole, Burton, MI

Makes 6 servings
Prep. Time: 30 minutes   ⚶   Cooking Time: 5–6 hours   ⚶   Ideal slow-cooker size: 6-qt.

1 lb. split peas, sorted and rinsed

2 qts. low-sodium vegetable broth

2 cups water

1 large onion, chopped

2 cloves garlic, minced

3 stalks celery, chopped

3 medium carrots, chopped finely

2 bay leaves

1 tsp. kosher salt

1 tsp. black pepper

1. Combine all ingredients and add to slow cooker.

2. Cover and cook on Low 5–6 hours. Remove bay leaves and serve.

TIP
If desired, add more salt after cooking, but note that this will increase sodium content.

Serving suggestion:
If creamy texture is desired, blend with immersion blender.

Calories: 230
Fat: 0g
Sodium: 580mg
Carbs: 56g
Sugar: 7g
Protein: 20g

Split Pea Soup

Phyllis Good, Lancaster, PA

Makes 8–10 servings

Prep. Time: 20 minutes ❧ Cooking Time: 4–8 hours ❧ Ideal slow-cooker size: 6-qt.

3 cups dried split peas (a little over 1 pound)
3 qts. water
½ tsp. garlic powder
½ tsp. dried oregano
1 cup diced, or thinly sliced, carrots
1 cup chopped celery
1 tsp. salt
¼–½ tsp. pepper (coarsely ground is great)
1 ham shank or hock

1. Put all ingredients into slow cooker, except the ham. Stir well.

2. Settle ham into mixture.

3. Cover. Cook on Low 4–8 hours, or until ham is tender and falling off the bone, and the peas are very soft.

4. Use a slotted spoon to lift the ham bone out of the soup. Allow it to cool until you can handle it without burning yourself.

5. Cut the ham into bite-sized pieces. Stir it back into the soup.

6. Heat the soup for 10 minutes, and then serve.

Calories: 287
Fat: 5g
Sodium: 595mg
Carbs: 38g
Sugar: 5g
Protein: 23g

Hearty Bean and Vegetable Soup

Jewel Showalter, Landisville, PA

Makes 8–10 servings

Prep. Time: 20–25 minutes ⚬ *Cooking Time: 6–8 hours* ⚬ *Ideal slow-cooker size: 5-qt.*

2 medium onions, sliced
2 cloves garlic, minced
2 Tbsp. olive oil
8 cups low-sodium vegetable broth
1 small head cabbage, chopped
2 large red potatoes, chopped
2 cups chopped celery
2 cups chopped carrots
4 cups corn
2 tsp. dried basil
1 tsp. dried marjoram
¼ tsp. dried oregano
1 tsp. salt
½ tsp. pepper
2 15-oz. cans navy beans, drained, rinsed

1. Sauté onions and garlic in oil in skillet. Transfer to large slow cooker.

2. Add remaining ingredients. Mix together well.

3. Cover. Cook on Low 6–8 hours.

Variation:

Add 2–3 cups cooked and cut-up chicken 30 minutes before serving if you wish.

Calories: 325
Fat: 5g
Sodium: 728mg
Carbs: 60g
Sugar: 11g
Protein: 13g

Butternut Squash Soup with Thai Gremolata

Andy Wagner, Quarryville, PA

Makes 4–6 servings
Prep. Time: 25 minutes   ♣   Cooking Time: 2–5 hours   ♣   Ideal slow-cooker size: 3½- or 4-qt.

2 lbs. butternut squash, peeled and cut into 1-inch pieces

2 cups vegetable broth

14-oz. can unsweetened coconut milk

¼ cup minced onions

1 Tbsp. brown sugar, packed

1 Tbsp. soy sauce or Bragg liquid aminos

½–1 tsp. crushed red pepper

2 Tbsp. lime juice

lime wedges, *optional*

Thai Gremolata:

½ cup chopped fresh basil or cilantro

½ cup chopped peanuts

1 Tbsp. finely shredded lime peel

1. In a 3½- or 4-qt. slow cooker, stir together squash, broth, coconut milk, onions, brown sugar, soy sauce, and crushed red pepper.

2. Cover and cook on Low for 4–5 hours or on High for 2–2½ hours.

3. Meanwhile, assemble the Thai Gremolata. Mix together basil, peanuts, and lime peel. Set aside.

4. Use an immersion or stand blender to carefully blend soup until completely smooth.

5. Stir in lime juice. Ladle into bowls and top with Thai Gremolata. If you wish, serve with lime wedges.

Calories: 285
Fat: 19g
Sodium: 600mg
Carbs: 31g
Sugar: 10.5g
Protein: 4g

Creamy Butternut Squash Soup

Hope Comerford, Clinton Township, MI

Makes 4–6 servings
Prep. Time: 20 minutes ⚜ Cooking Time: 8 hours ⚜ Ideal slow-cooker size: 3-qt.

1 ½ lb. butternut squash, peeled and cut into 1-inch chunks

1 small onion, quartered

1 carrot, cut into 1-inch chunks

1 small sweet potato, cut into 1-inch chunks

¼ tsp. cinnamon

⅛ tsp. nutmeg

½ tsp. sugar

¼ tsp. salt

⅛ tsp. pepper

⅛ tsp. ginger

3 cups vegetable stock (or you can use chicken stock)

1 cup half-and-half

1. Place the butternut squash, onion, carrot, and sweet potato pieces into your crock.

2. Sprinkle the contents of the crock with the cinnamon, nutmeg, sugar, salt, pepper, and ginger. Pour the stock over the top.

3. Cover and cook on Low for 8 hours, or until the vegetables are soft.

4. Using an immersion blender, blend the soup until smooth.

5. Remove ¼ cup of the soup and mix it with 1 cup of half-and-half. Pour this into the crock and mix until well combined.

Calories: 171
Fat: 6g
Sodium: 297mg
Carbs: 26g
Sugar: 8g
Protein: 6g

Potato Leek Soup

Melissa Paskvan, Novi, MI

Makes 4–6 servings
Prep. Time: 20 minutes　☙　Cooking Time: 6 hours　☙　Ideal slow-cooker size: 6-qt.

3 large leeks, chopped (rinse leek well and include the tough tops)

5 medium Yukon Gold potatoes, chopped

2 cups vegetable stock

2 cups water

2–3 bay leaves

½ head cauliflower, broken up

3 stalks celery, whole

¼ tsp. pepper

salt, to taste

1. Place all of the ingredients in the slow cooker and put the tough tops of the leeks on the top.

2. Cover and cook on Low for 6 hours.

3. Remove tough leek tops, celery, and bay leaves. Either blend all the ingredients in a blender or use an immersion blender while in the crock and blend until very creamy. Salt to taste and add water if too thick for your liking.

Serving suggestion:

Serve with scallions on top for a vegan option, with Monterey Jack cheese and scallions for a vegetarian option, or with bacon bits, scallions, and cheese for a meat-eater option.

Calories: 170
Fat: 0g
Sodium: 275mg
Carbs: 38g
Sugar: 5g
Protein: 6g

Easy Potato Soup

Yvonne Kauffman Boettger, Harrisonburg, VA

Makes 8 servings
Prep. Time: 10 minutes   ॐ   Cooking Time: 5 hours   ॐ   Ideal slow-cooker size: 4- to 6-qt.

3 cups chicken broth

2-lb. bag frozen hash brown potatoes

1½ tsp. salt

¾ tsp. pepper

3 cups low-fat milk

3 cups shredded low-fat Monterey Jack or cheddar cheese

1. Place chicken broth, potatoes, salt, and pepper in slow cooker.

2. Cover and cook on High 4 hours, or until potatoes are soft.

3. Leaving the broth and potatoes in the slow cooker, mash the potatoes lightly, leaving some larger chunks.

4. Add milk and cheese. Blend in thoroughly.

5. Cover and cook on High until cheese melts and soup is hot, about an hour.

Calories: 486
Fat: 25g
Sodium: 1399mg
Carbs: 45g
Sugar: 7g
Protein: 20g

Creamy Potato Soup

Hope Comerford, Clinton Township, MI

Makes 6 servings
Prep. Time: 20 minutes   ⚶   Cooking Time: 8–10 hours   ⚶   Ideal slow-cooker size: 5-qt.

8–9 Idaho potatoes, chopped into bite-sized pieces

4½ cups low-sodium chicken broth or stock

½ cup low-fat milk

1 medium onion, chopped

2–4 carrots, chopped

1–2 stalks celery, chopped

3 green onions, chopped

8-oz. block reduced-fat cream cheese, chopped into cubes

¼ cup nonfat plain Greek yogurt

3 Tbsp. cornstarch

2 Tbsp. butter

2 tsp. garlic powder

1 tsp. onion powder

1½ tsp. pepper

1 tsp. salt

1. Place all ingredients into your crock and stir.

2. Cook on Low for 8–10 hours.

Serving suggestion:
Serve with fresh chopped chives or green onions on top and little bit of shredded cheese.

TIP
Use an immersion blender to give your soup a smoother and creamier texture.

Calories: 312
Fat: 11g
Sodium: 1130mg
Carbs: 40g
Sugar: 9g
Protein: 13g

Minestrone

Bernita Boyts, Shawnee Mission, KS

Makes 8–10 servings
Prep. Time: 15 minutes & Cooking Time: 4–9 hours & Ideal slow-cooker size: 3½- to 4-qt.

1 large onion, chopped

4 carrots, sliced

3 stalks celery, sliced

2 cloves garlic, minced

1 Tbsp. olive oil

6-oz. can tomato paste

2 cups low-sodium chicken, beef, or vegetable broth

24-oz. can pinto beans, drained, rinsed

10-oz. pkg. frozen green beans

2–3 cups chopped cabbage

1 medium zucchini, sliced

8 cups water

2 Tbsp. parsley

2 Tbsp. Italian seasoning

1 tsp. sea salt, or more to taste

½ tsp. pepper

¾ cup dry *acini di pepe* (small round pasta)

grated Parmesan, or Asiago, cheese, *optional*

1. Sauté onion, carrots, celery, and garlic in oil in skillet until tender. Add to slow cooker.

2. Combine all other ingredients, except pasta and cheese, in slow cooker.

3. Cover. Cook 4–5 hours on High or 8–9 hours on Low.

4. Add pasta 1 hour before cooking is complete.

5. Top individual servings with cheese, if desired.

Calories: 205
Fat: 3g
Sodium: 478mg
Carbs: 37g
Sugar: 10g
Protein: 11g

Enchilada Soup

Melissa Paskvan, Novi, MI

Makes 6–8 servings
Prep. Time: 5 minutes ⚜ *Cooking Time: 6–8 hours* ⚜ *Ideal slow-cooker size: 6-qt.*

14½-oz. can diced tomatoes with green chilies or chipotle

12-oz. jar enchilada sauce

4 cups vegetable broth

1 small onion, chopped

3 cups sliced tricolor bell peppers

10-oz. pkg. frozen corn

1 cup water

½ cup uncooked quinoa

1. Add all ingredients to slow cooker.

2. Cover and cook on Low for 6–8 hours.

Calories: 150
Fat: 2g
Sodium: 830mg
Carbs: 28g
Sugar: 7g
Protein: 4g

STEWS

Slow-Cooker Beef Stew

Becky Fixel, Grosse Pointe Farms, MI

Makes 8–10 servings

Prep. Time: 30 minutes   ♣   Cooking Time: 6 hours   ♣   Ideal slow-cooker size: 3-qt.

2 lbs. stew beef, cubed

¼ cup white rice flour

1½ tsp. salt

½ tsp. black pepper

32 oz. beef broth

1 onion, diced

1 tsp. Worcestershire sauce

1 bay leaf

1 tsp. paprika

4 carrots, sliced

3 potatoes, sliced thinly

1 stalk celery, sliced

1. Place the meat in crock.

2. Mix the flour, salt, and pepper. Pour over the meat and mix well. Make sure to cover the meat with flour.

3. Add broth to the crock and stir well.

4. Add remaining ingredients and stir to mix well.

5. Cook on High for at least 5 hours, then on Low for 1 hour. Remove bay leaf and serve.

Calories: 250

Fat: 4.5g

Sodium: 860mg

Carbs: 27g

Sugar: 1.5g

Protein: 26g

Colorful Beef Stew

Hope Comerford, Clinton Township, MI

Makes 6 servings
Prep. Time: 20 minutes ⚜ *Cooking Time: 8–9 hours* ⚜ *Ideal slow-cooker size: 4-qt.*

2 lbs. boneless beef chuck roast, trimmed of fat and cut into ¾-inch pieces

1 large red onion, chopped

2 cups low-sodium beef broth

6-oz. can tomato paste

4 cloves garlic, minced

1 Tbsp. paprika

2 tsp. dried marjoram

½ tsp. black pepper

1 tsp. sea salt

1 red bell pepper, sliced

1 yellow bell pepper, sliced

1 orange bell pepper, sliced

1. Place all ingredients except the sliced bell peppers in the crock, and stir.

2. Cover and cook on Low for 8–9 hours. Stir in sliced bell peppers during the last 45 minutes of cooking time.

Calories: 443
Fat: 15g
Sodium: 180mg
Carbs: 15g
Sugar: 7g
Protein: 50g

Stay-in-Bed Stew

Janie Steele, Moore, OK
Judy Newman, Saint Marys, ON, Canada

Makes 6 servings
Prep. Time: 20 minutes ⚜ *Cooking Time: 5–6 hours* ⚜ *Ideal slow-cooker size: 3-qt.*

1 lb. chuck stewing meat
1 large onion, cut in chunks
2 potatoes, peeled and diced large
4 carrots, peeled and sliced
15-oz. can tomato sauce
½ cup water
¼ tsp. pepper
2 tsp. kosher salt
2 tsp. minced garlic
1 bay leaf
1 cup frozen peas

1. Put all ingredients except peas in slow cooker.

2. Cover. Cook on Low 5–6 hours, or until vegetables are as tender as you like them.

3. Add peas 30 minutes before serving.

4. Remove bay leaf before serving.

Calories: 186
Fat: 4g
Sodium: 824mg
Carbs: 19g
Sugar: 4g
Protein: 20g

Nutritious Tasty Beef Stew

Annie Boshart, Lititz, PA

Makes 12 servings
Prep. Time: 30 minutes   ❧   Cooking Time: 4 hours   ❧   Ideal slow-cooker size: 6-qt.

3-lb. rump roast, or your choice of beef

4 carrots, cut into serving-sized pieces

8 potatoes, peeled and cut into bite-sized pieces

¼ cup chopped red onion

¼ cup chopped white onion

2 cups fresh salsa

2 Tbsp. instant tapioca

1 Tbsp. Worcestershire sauce

1. Place rump roast or choice of beef in slow cooker.

2. Add the vegetables to slow cooker.

3. Mix together the salsa, tapioca, and Worcestershire sauce. Pour on top of vegetables.

4. Cover and cook on High for 4 hours.

TIP
Fresh salsa is made with fresh herbs, tomatoes, and other desired ingredients—vinegar, lemon juice, and cilantro to taste. This can also be frozen or canned.

Calories: 293
Fat: 5g
Sodium: 433mg
Carbs: 30g
Sugar: 5g
Protein: 29g

Moroccan Beef Stew

Joyce Cox, Port Angeles, WA

Makes 4–6 servings
Prep. Time: 30 minutes ⚜ *Cooking Time: 8–10 hours* ⚜ *Ideal slow-cooker size: 4-qt.*

3 Tbsp. olive oil, *divided*

2 cups thinly sliced onion

5 cloves garlic, minced

2-lb. beef chuck roast, cut into 2-inch cubes, seasoned with salt and pepper

15-oz. can diced tomatoes with juice

1 cup low-sodium beef broth

1 Tbsp. honey

2 tsp. ground cumin

2 tsp. ground coriander

1 tsp. ground ginger

1 tsp. ground turmeric

1 cinnamon stick

1 bay leaf

black pepper, to taste

1 cup pitted, chopped prunes

1. Heat 1½ Tbsp. olive oil in large frying pan and sauté onions until golden brown. Add garlic and cook 1 more minute. Transfer to slow cooker.

2. Heat remaining 1½ Tbsp. oil in pan. Sear beef cubes on all sides. Transfer to slow cooker.

3. Add rest of ingredients to slow cooker. Stir well.

4. Cover and cook on Low for 8–10 hours. Remove cinnamon stick and bay leaf before serving.

Serving suggestion:

Serve over brown rice or quinoa.

Calories: 410
Fat: 19g
Sodium: 310mg
Carbs: 39g
Sugar: 22g
Protein: 18g

Pirate Stew

Nancy Graves, Manhattan, KS

Makes 4–6 servings

Prep. Time: 15 minutes ⚬ Cooking Time: 6 hours ⚬ Ideal slow-cooker size: 4-qt.

¾ cup sliced onion

1 lb. extra-lean ground beef

¼ cup uncooked, long-grain rice

3 cups diced raw potatoes

1 cup diced celery

2 cups canned kidney beans, drained, rinsed

1 tsp. salt

⅛ tsp. pepper

¼ tsp. chili powder

¼ tsp. Worcestershire sauce

1 cup tomato sauce

½ cup water

1. Brown onion and ground beef in skillet. Drain.

2. Layer ingredients in slow cooker in order given.

3. Cover. Cook on Low 6 hours, or until potatoes and rice are cooked.

Calories: 296
Fat: 6g
Sodium: 594mg
Carbs: 36g
Sugar: 4g
Protein: 24g

Moroccan Spiced Stew

Melissa Paskvan, Novi, MI

Makes 6–8 servings
Prep. Time: 10 minutes & Cooking Time: 8 hours & Ideal slow-cooker size: 5-qt.

3 cups canned chopped tomatoes

3 cups chicken stock

1 lb. lamb (ground or stew-cut pieces)

1 medium onion, chopped

⅛ tsp. fresh grated ginger

1½ tsp. cumin

¾ tsp. cinnamon

¾ tsp. turmeric

⅛–¼ tsp. cayenne pepper

½ cup shredded or chopped carrots

3 cups chopped sweet potato

salt and pepper, to taste

1. Place all ingredients in the crock and mix well to incorporate the spices.

2. Cover and cook on Low for 8 hours.

Serving suggestion:

Top with harissa for a zesty, warm flavor. Ladle this stew over brown rice or millet for a filling meal. Cook with ½ cup dried apricots or dates to impart a sweet taste.

TIP

If you really want to seal in the warm spices, add 1 Tbsp. olive oil to a pan and brown just the outsides of the lamb pieces and cook with onions and spices. Then add in about 1 cup of the chicken stock to deglaze the pan and pour all ingredients from the pan to the slow cooker and add the remaining ingredients. This can also be made vegan using quinoa and chickpeas for the protein and substituting with vegetable stock. I add ½ cup rinsed quinoa to the recipe and 1 can garbanzo beans (chickpeas).

Calories: 330
Fat: 19g
Sodium: 415mg
Carbs: 225.5g
Sugar: 9.5g
Protein: 16g

Zucchini Stew

Colleen Heatwole, Burton, MI

Makes 6 servings
Prep. Time: 30 minutes   ⚜   Cooking Time: 4–6 hours   ⚜   Ideal slow-cooker size: 6-qt.

1 lb. Italian turkey sausage, sliced

2 stalks celery, diced

2 medium green bell peppers, diced

1 medium onion, chopped

2 28-oz. cans diced tomatoes

2 lbs. zucchini, cut into ½-inch slices

2 cloves garlic, minced

1 tsp. sugar

1 tsp. dried oregano

1 tsp. Italian seasoning

1 tsp. sea salt, *optional* (taste first)

6 Tbsp. grated Parmesan cheese, *optional*

1. Brown sausage in hot skillet until brown and crumbly, about 5–7 minutes. Drain and discard grease.

2. Mix celery, bell peppers, and onion into cooked sausage and cook and stir until they are softened, 10–12 minutes.

3. Combine remaining ingredients, except Parmesan cheese, and add to slow cooker.

4. Cook on Low 4–6 hours. Garnish each serving with 1 Tbsp. Parmesan cheese if desired.

Calories: 230
Fat: 7g
Sodium: 954mg
Carbs: 24g
Sugar: 9g
Protein: 17g

Chili Chicken Stew with Rice

Jenny R. Unternahrer, Wayland, IA

Makes 4–5 servings
Prep. Time: 30 minutes ⚜ Cooking Time: 2½–5 hours ⚜ Ideal slow-cooker size: 2½-qt.

1½ lbs. chicken tenders*

½ small onion, diced

15-oz. can black beans, drained, rinsed

14½-oz. can petite diced tomatoes, undrained

1 cup whole corn, drained if needed (thawed if frozen)

2 tsp. chili powder

½ tsp. cumin

2–4 dashes cayenne pepper

1½ tsp. salt

2 cups cooked brown rice

nonfat plain Greek yogurt, *optional*

shredded Mexican blend cheese, *optional*

* You can try whole boneless, skinless chicken breast, but allow more time to cook.

1. Add all the ingredients, except brown rice, yogurt, and shredded cheese, to crock.

2. Mix. Cover and cook on High for 2½ hours or Low for 5 hours.

3. Shred chicken; stir to incorporate.

4. Serve over brown rice and add desired amount of nonfat plain Greek yogurt and shredded Mexican blend cheese, if desired.

Calories: 400
Fat: 5g
Sodium: 651mg
Carbs: 47g
Sugar: 4g
Protein: 41g

Apple Chicken Stew

Lorraine Pflederer, Goshen, IN

Makes 4 servings
Prep. Time: 30–40 minutes   &   Cooking Time: 4–5 hours   &   Ideal slow-cooker size: 5-qt.

4 medium potatoes, cubed

4 medium carrots, sliced ¼-inch thick

1 medium red onion, halved and sliced

1 stalk celery, thinly sliced

1½ tsp. salt

¾ tsp. dried thyme

½ tsp. pepper

¼–½ tsp. caraway seeds

2 lbs. boneless, skinless chicken breasts, cubed

1 large tart apple, peeled and cubed

½ cup apple cider

¾ cup water

1 Tbsp. apple cider vinegar

1 bay leaf

minced fresh parsley

1. Layer potatoes, carrots, onion, and celery into slow cooker.

2. In a small bowl, combine salt, thyme, pepper, and caraway seeds. Sprinkle half over vegetables.

3. Add the chicken and apple.

4. In another small bowl, combine apple cider, water, and vinegar. Pour over chicken and apple.

5. Sprinkle with remaining seasoning mixture. Lay bay leaf on top.

6. Cover. Cook on High 4–5 hours, or until vegetables are tender and chicken juices run clear.

7. Discard bay leaf. Stir before serving.

8. Sprinkle individual serving bowls with parsley.

Calories: 427
Fat: 6g
Sodium: 895mg
Carbs: 34g
Sugar: 10g
Protein: 54g

Chicken, Pumpkin and Chickpea Stew

Andrea Maher, Dunedin, FL

Makes 6 servings
Prep. Time: 10 minutes ⚬ *Cooking Time: 3–8 hours* ⚬ *Ideal slow-cooker size: 5- or 6-qt.*

24 oz. boneless skinless chicken breasts, cut thin

3 cups canned pumpkin puree

2 cups chickpeas

3 cups mushrooms

1½ cups low-sodium chicken broth

1½ cups plain nonfat Greek yogurt

salt, to taste

pepper, to taste

cinnamon, to taste

red pepper and chili powder, to taste, *optional*

1. Add all ingredients to slow cooker.

2. Cook on High 3–4 hours or Low 6–8.

TIP
This soup freezes well, so it's easy to freeze in portion-sized containers.

Calories: 275
Fat: 10g
Sodium: 230mg
Carbs: 28g
Sugar: 7g
Protein: 36g

CHILIES

Slow-Cooker Chili

Kay Magruder, Seminole, OK

Makes 8–10 servings
Prep. Time: 25 minutes ☙ Cooking Time: 6–12 hours ☙ Ideal slow-cooker size: 6-qt.

3 lbs. stewing meat

2 cloves garlic, minced

¼ tsp. pepper

½ tsp. cumin

¼ tsp. dry mustard

7½-oz. can jalapeño relish

1 cup low-sodium beef broth

1–1½ onions, according to your taste preference, chopped

½ tsp. salt

½ tsp. dried oregano

1 Tbsp. chili powder

7-oz. can green chilies, chopped

14½-oz. can stewed tomatoes, chopped

15-oz. can tomato sauce

2 15-oz. cans red kidney beans, rinsed and drained

2 15-oz. cans pinto beans, rinsed and drained

1. Combine all ingredients except kidney and pinto beans in slow cooker.

2. Cover. Cook on Low 10–12 hours or on High 6–7 hours. Add beans halfway through cooking time.

Calories: 507
Fat: 13g
Sodium: 512mg
Carbs: 51g
Sugar: 5g
Protein: 46g

Our Favorite Chili

Ruth Shank, Gridley, IL

Makes 10–12 servings
Prep. Time: 20 minutes ⚶ *Cooking Time: 4–10 hours* ⚶ *Ideal slow-cooker size: 5-qt.*

1½ lbs. extra-lean ground beef

¼ cup chopped onions

1 stalk celery, chopped

extra-virgin olive oil, *optional*

29-oz. can stewed tomatoes

2 15½-oz. cans red kidney beans, drained, rinsed

2 16-oz. cans chili beans, undrained

½ cup ketchup

1½ tsp. lemon juice

2 tsp. vinegar

1 tsp. brown sugar

1½ tsp. kosher salt

1 tsp. Worcestershire sauce

½ tsp. garlic powder

½ tsp. dry mustard powder

1 Tbsp. chili powder

2 6-oz. cans tomato paste

1. Brown ground beef, onions, and celery in oil (if using) in skillet. Stir frequently to break up clumps of meat. When meat is no longer pink, drain off drippings.

2. Place meat and vegetables in slow cooker. Add all remaining ingredients. Mix well.

3. Cover. Cook on Low 8–10 hours or on High 4–5 hours.

Calories: 364
Fat: 7g
Sodium: 930mg
Carbs: 50g
Sugar: 8g
Protein: 27g

Hearty Chili

Joylynn Keener, Lancaster, PA

Makes 8 servings
Prep. Time: 20–25 minutes   &   Cooking Time: 8 hours   &   Ideal slow-cooker size: 5-qt.

1 onion, chopped

2 stalks celery, chopped

1 lb. extra-lean ground beef

2 14-oz. cans kidney beans, drained, rinsed

14-oz. can pinto beans, drained, rinsed

14-oz. can diced tomatoes

2 14-oz. cans tomato sauce

1 green bell pepper, chopped

1 Tbsp. turbinado sugar

1 tsp. salt

1 tsp. dried thyme

1 tsp. dried oregano

1 Tbsp. chili powder, or to taste

1. Brown onion, celery, and beef in skillet. Stir frequently to break up clumps of meat. When meat is no longer pink, drain off drippings.

2. Spoon meat into slow cooker. Stir in all remaining ingredients, mixing well.

3. Cover. Cook on Low 8 hours.

Calories: 265
Fat: 5g
Sodium: 829mg
Carbs: 37g
Sugar: 6g
Protein: 19g

Chicken Chili

Sharon Miller, Holmesville, OH

Makes 6 servings
Prep. Time: 15 minutes ⚬ *Cooking Time: 5–6 hours* ⚬ *Ideal slow-cooker size: 4-qt.*

2 lbs. boneless, skinless chicken breasts, cubed

1 Tbsp. butter

2 14-oz. cans diced tomatoes, undrained

15-oz. can red kidney beans, rinsed and drained

1 cup diced onion

1 cup diced red bell pepper

1–2 Tbsp. chili powder, according to your taste preference

1 tsp. cumin

1 tsp. dried oregano

Salt and pepper, to taste

1. In skillet on high heat, brown chicken cubes in butter until they have some browned edges. Place in greased slow cooker.

2. Pour one of the cans of tomatoes with its juice into skillet to get all the browned bits and butter. Scrape and pour into slow cooker.

3. Add rest of ingredients, including other can of tomatoes, to cooker.

4. Cook on Low for 5–6 hours.

Calories: 329
Fat: 5g
Sodium: 320mg
Carbs: 27g
Sugar: 3g
Protein: 41g

White Chili

Rebecca Plank Leichty, Harrisonburg, VA

Makes 6–8 servings
Prep. Time: 15 minutes ⚜ *Cooking Time: 4–10 hours* ⚜ *Ideal slow-cooker size: 5-qt.*

15-oz. can chickpeas, or garbanzo
beans, drained, rinsed

15-oz. can small northern beans,
drained, rinsed

15-oz. can pinto beans, drained, rinsed

1 qt. frozen corn, or 2 1-lb. bags frozen
corn

1½ cups shredded cooked chicken

2 Tbsp. minced onions

1 red bell pepper, diced

3 tsp. minced garlic

3 tsp. ground cumin

½ tsp. salt

½ tsp. dried oregano

4 cups low-sodium chicken broth

1. Combine all ingredients in slow cooker.

2. Cover. Cook on Low 8–10 hours or on High 4–5 hours.

Variation:

For more zip, add 2 tsp. chili powder, or one or more chopped jalapeño peppers, to Step 1.

Calories: 393
Fat: 5g
Sodium: 523mg
Carbs: 59g
Sugar: 12g
Protein: 33g

White Bean and Chicken Chili

Hope Comerford, Clinton Township, MI

Makes 6–8 servings

Prep. Time: 15 minutes ⚘ *Cooking Time: 8–10 hours* ⚘ *Ideal slow-cooker size: 5-qt.*

2 lbs. boneless, skinless chicken, cut into bite-sized chunks

½ cup dry navy beans, soaked overnight, drained, and rinsed

½ cup dry great northern beans, soaked overnight, drained, and rinsed

½ cup chopped carrots

1½ cups chopped onion

2 14½-oz. cans petite diced tomatoes

5 cloves garlic, minced

6-oz. can tomato paste

1 Tbsp. cumin

1 Tbsp. chili powder

1 tsp. salt

¼ tsp. pepper

8 cups low-sodium chicken stock

1. Place all ingredients into the crock and stir to mix well.

2. Cover and cook on Low for 8–10 hours.

Calories: 371
Fat: 7g
Sodium: 991mg
Carbs: 38g
Sugar: 10g
Protein: 39g

Southwestern Chili

Colleen Heatwole, Burton, MI

Makes 12 servings
Prep. Time: 30 minutes ⚹ *Cooking Time: 6–8 hours* ⚹ *Ideal slow-cooker size: 6- or 7-qt.*

32-oz. can whole tomatoes

15-oz. jar salsa

15-oz. can low-sodium chicken broth

1 cup barley

3 cups water

1 tsp. chili powder

1 tsp. ground cumin

15-oz. can black beans

15-oz. can whole kernel corn

3 cups chopped cooked chicken

1 cup low-fat shredded cheddar cheese, *optional*

low-fat sour cream, *optional*

1. Combine all ingredients in slow cooker except for cheese and sour cream.

2. Cover and cook on Low for 6–8 hours.

3. Serve with cheese and sour cream on each bowl, if desired.

Calories: 300
Fat: 7g
Sodium: 650mg
Carbs: 39.5g
Sugar: 6g
Protein: 22.5g

Chipotle Chili

Janie Steele, Moore, OK

Makes 6–8 servings
Prep. Time: 30 minutes ❧ *Cooking Time: 3–6 hours* ❧ *Ideal slow-cooker size: 3- or 4-qt.*

2 cloves garlic, chopped

1¼ lbs. boneless, skinless chicken thighs, cubed

1 lb. butternut squash, peeled and cubed

15-oz. can pinto beans, rinsed and drained

juice and zest of ½ orange

2–3 chipotle peppers in adobo sauce, minced

2 Tbsp. tomato paste

2 green onions, sliced, chopped

cilantro, *optional*

1. Combine garlic, chicken, squash, beans, orange juice, orange zest, peppers, and tomato paste in slow cooker.

2. Cook 3–4 hours on High or 5–6 hours on Low until chicken is done.

3. Mash some of the stew with potato masher to make it thicker.

4. Stir in green onions and, if using, cilantro. Serve hot.

Calories: 210
Fat: 7g
Sodium: 260mg
Carbs: 20g
Sugar: 3g
Protein: 22g

White and Green Chili

Hope Comerford, Clinton Township, MI

Makes 6 servings
Prep. Time: 20 minutes & Cooking Time: 7–8 hours & Ideal slow-cooker size: 4-qt.

1 lb. lean ground turkey, browned

1 cup chopped onion

2 15-oz. cans great northern beans, drained and rinsed

1 16-oz. jar salsa verde (green salsa)

2 cups chicken broth

4-oz. can green chilies

1½ tsp. ground cumin

1 tsp. sea salt

¼ tsp. black pepper

2 Tbsp. chopped fresh cilantro

⅓ cup nonfat plain Greek yogurt, *optional*

1. Place all ingredients in crock except cilantro and Greek yogurt. Stir.

2. Cover and cook on Low for 7–8 hours. Stir in cilantro. Serve each bowl of chili with a dollop of the Greek yogurt, if using.

Serving suggestion:

Garnish with diced jalapeño peppers.

Calories: 325
Fat: 8g
Sodium: 1730mg
Carbs: 38g
Sugar: 6.5g
Protein: 26.5g

Pumpkin Chili

Hope Comerford, Clinton Township, MI

Makes 8 servings
Prep. Time: 10 minutes ⚬ Cooking Time: 7–8 hours ⚬ Ideal slow-cooker size: 6-qt.

16-oz. can kidney beans, drained and rinsed

16-oz. can black beans, drained and rinsed

1 large onion, chopped

½ green pepper, chopped

1 lb. ground turkey, browned

15-oz. can pumpkin puree

4 cups chopped fresh tomatoes

3 Tbsp. garlic powder

1 Tbsp. ancho chili powder

1 tsp. salt

2 tsp. cumin

¼ tsp. pepper

4 Tbsp. beef bouillon granules

5 cups water

1. Place the kidney beans, black beans, onion, and pepper in the crock.

2. Crumble the ground turkey over the top and spoon the pumpkin puree on top of that.

3. Add in the remaining ingredients and stir.

4. Cover and cook on Low for 7–8 hours.

Serving suggestion:
Garnish with pumpkin seeds.

Calories: 300
Fat: 7g
Sodium: 650mg
Carbs: 39.5g
Sugar: 6g
Protein: 22.5g

Black Bean Chili

Kenda Autumn, San Francisco, CA

Makes 6–8 servings
Prep. Time: 15 minutes ❧ Cooking Time: 8 hours ❧ Ideal slow-cooker size: 5-qt.

1 Tbsp. olive oil
1 medium onion, chopped
1 tsp. ground cumin
1 tsp. ground coriander
1 Tbsp. chili powder
1 tsp. garam masala
16-oz. can black beans, rinsed and drained
14-oz. can diced tomatoes
1 sweet potato, cubed
2 cups cubed butternut squash
1 cup corn

1. Heat oil in saucepan. Brown onion, cumin, coriander, chili powder, and garam masala.

2. Transfer to slow cooker.

3. Add beans, tomatoes, sweet potato, butternut squash, and corn.

4. Cook on Low 8 hours.

TIP

Use this recipe as a starting point for chili. I add other vegetables in step 3 that I have on hand, such as red bell pepper and mushrooms.

Calories: 240
Fat: 4g
Sodium: 300mg
Carbs: 46g
Sugar: 5g
Protein: 9g

Wintertime Vegetable Chili

Maricarol Magill, Freehold, NJ

Makes 6 servings
Prep. Time: 20 minutes ⚜ Cooking Time: 6–8 hours ⚜ Ideal slow-cooker size: 6-qt.

1 medium butternut squash, peeled and cubed

2 medium carrots, peeled and diced

1 medium onion, diced

3 tsp.–3 Tbsp. chili powder, depending on how hot you like your chili

2 14-oz. cans diced tomatoes

4¼-oz. can chopped mild green chilies, drained

1 tsp. salt, *optional*

1 cup vegetable broth

2 16-oz. cans black beans, drained and rinsed

nonfat plain Greek yogurt, *optional*

1. In slow cooker, layer all ingredients, except yogurt, in order given.

2. Cover. Cook on Low 6–8 hours, or until vegetables are as tender as you want.

3. Stir before serving.

4. Top individual servings with dollops of nonfat plain Greek yogurt, if desired.

Calories: 352
Fat: 2g
Sodium: 355mg
Carbs: 55g
Sugar: 12g
Protein: 19g

Main Dishes

Chuck Roast

Janie Steele, Moore, OK

Makes 6–8 servings
Prep. Time: 20 minutes ⚜ Cooking Time: 8 hours ⚜ Ideal slow-cooker size: 5-qt.

¼ cup flour

salt and pepper, to taste

3–4-pound boneless chuck roast

10 pepperoncini, fresh or jarred

2 Tbsp. mayonnaise

2 tsp. apple cider vinegar

¼ tsp. dried dill

⅛ tsp. paprika

1. Mix flour, salt, and pepper and rub into roast. Place roast in crock.

2. Top with pepperoncini.

3. In a small bowl mix mayonnaise, vinegar, dill, and paprika. Spread over meat.

4. Cover and cook on Low for 8 hours. Remove from cooker, shred with forks, and return to cooker. Stir to mix juices and serve.

Calories: 303
Fat: 15g
Sodium: 318mg
Carbs: 4g
Sugar: 0g
Protein: 37g

Spicy Beef Roast

Karen Ceneviva, Seymour, CT

Makes 10 servings

Prep. Time: 15–20 minutes ⚜ *Cooking Time: 3–8 hours* ⚜ *Ideal slow-cooker size: 4- or 5-qt.*

1–2 Tbsp. cracked black peppercorns

2 cloves garlic, minced

3-lb. eye round roast, trimmed of fat

3 Tbsp. balsamic vinegar

¼ cup gluten-free reduced-sodium soy sauce or Bragg liquid aminos

2 Tbsp. Worcestershire sauce

2 tsp. dry mustard

1. Rub cracked pepper and garlic onto roast. Put roast in slow cooker.

2. Make several shallow slits in top of meat.

3. In a small bowl, combine remaining ingredients. Spoon over meat.

4. Cover and cook on Low for 6–8 hours, or on High for 3–4 hours, just until meat is tender, but not dry.

Calories: 240

Fat: 6g

Sodium: 530mg

Carbs: 2g

Sugar: 1g

Protein: 41.5g

Low-Fat Slow-Cooker Roast

Charlotte Shaffer, East Earl, PA

Makes 10 servings
Prep. Time: 15 minutes ⚶ Cooking Time: 3–8 hours ⚶ Ideal slow-cooker size: 6-qt.

3-lb. boneless beef roast

4 carrots, peeled and cut into 2-inch pieces

4 potatoes, cut into quarters

2 onions, quartered

1 cup low-sodium beef broth or stock

1 tsp. garlic powder

1 tsp. Mrs. Dash Original Blend seasoning

½ tsp. salt

½ tsp. black pepper

1. Place roast in slow cooker.

2. Add carrots around edges, pushing them down so they reach the bottom of the crock.

3. Add potatoes and onions.

4. Mix together broth and seasonings and pour over roast.

5. Cover and cook on Low for 6–8 hours, or on High for 3–4 hours.

Calories: 340
Fat: 12g
Sodium: 275mg
Carbs: 20g
Sugar: 3g
Protein: 39g

Espresso-Braised Beef

Dena Mell-Dorchy, Royal Oak, MI

Makes 6 servings

Prep. Time: 25 minutes ⚬ *Cooking Time: 8–9 hours* ⚬ *Ideal slow-cooker size: 3- or 4-qt.*

I large onion, cut into wedges

3 medium carrots, cut into ½-inch pieces

I medium turnip, cut into 1-inch pieces

3 stalks celery, cut into 1-inch pieces

1½ lbs. boneless beef chuck, cut into 1-inch pieces

⅔ cup beef stock

2 Tbsp. tomato paste

I Tbsp. instant espresso powder

I tsp. packed brown sugar

I tsp. dried thyme

I tsp. dried rosemary

½ tsp. sea salt

¼ tsp. pepper

1. Spray slow cooker with nonstick cooking spray.

2. In crock, combine onion, carrots, turnip, and celery. Top with beef.

3. Whisk together stock, tomato paste, espresso powder, brown sugar, thyme, rosemary, salt, and pepper. Pour over beef and vegetables in crock.

4. Cover and cook on Low for 8–9 hours.

Serving suggestion:
Serve over cooked brown rice or quinoa.

Calories: 240
Fat: 12.5g
Sodium: 370mg
Carbs: 10g
Sugar: 5g
Protein: 23.5g

Chianti-Braised Short Ribs

Veronica Sabo, Shelton, CT

Makes 8 servings
Prep. Time: 30–40 minutes ⚜ Cooking Time: 6 hours ⚜ Ideal slow-cooker size: 5- or 6-qt.

8 meaty beef short ribs on bone (4–5 lbs.)

salt, to taste

pepper, to taste

1 Tbsp. olive oil

1 onion, finely chopped

2 cups Chianti wine

2 tomatoes, seeded and chopped

1 tsp. tomato paste

salt, to taste

pepper, to taste

1. Season ribs with salt and pepper.

2. Add olive oil to large skillet. Brown half the ribs 7–10 minutes, turning to brown all sides. Drain and remove to slow cooker.

3. Repeat browning with second half of ribs. Drain and transfer to slow cooker.

4. Pour off all but one tablespoon drippings from skillet.

5. Sauté onion in skillet, scraping up any browned bits, until slightly softened, about 4 minutes.

6. Add wine and tomatoes to skillet. Bring to a boil.

7. Carefully pour hot mixture into slow cooker.

8. Cover. Cook on Low 6 hours, or until ribs are tender.

9. Transfer ribs to serving plate and cover to keep warm.

10. Strain cooking liquid from slow cooker into a measuring cup.

11. Skim off as much fat as possible.

12. Pour remaining juice into skillet used to brown ribs. Boil sauce until reduced to one cup.

13. Stir in tomato paste until smooth.

14. Season to taste with salt and pepper.

15. Serve sauce over ribs or on the side.

Calories: 250
Fat: 13g
Sodium: 45mg
Carbs: 5g
Sugar: 2g
Protein: 18g

Swiss Steak with Carrots and Tomatoes

Becky Harder, Monument, CO

Makes 6 servings
Prep. Time: 25 minutes & Cooking Time: 5–7 hours & Ideal slow-cooker size: 4- or 5-qt.

2-lb. lean beef round steak, cut 1-inch thick

¼ cup flour

1 tsp. kosher salt

1 stalk celery, chopped

2 carrots, pared and chopped

¼ cup chopped onions

½ tsp. Worcestershire sauce

2 cups whole tomatoes

½–1 cup low-sodium tomato juice

½ cup grated, low-fat, low-sodium American cheese, *optional*

1. Cut steak into six serving pieces. Dredge in flour mixed with salt. Place in slow cooker.

2. Add chopped vegetables and Worcestershire sauce.

3. Pour tomatoes and juice over meat and vegetables.

4. Cover. Cook on Low 5–7 hours.

5. Just before serving, sprinkle with grated cheese, if desired.

Calories: 270
Fat: 8g
Sodium: 690mg
Carbs: 11g
Sugar: 5g
Protein: 37g

Swiss Steak with Onion, Peppers, and Tomatoes

Nadine Martinitz, Salina, KS
Hazel L. Propst, Oxford, PA

Makes 10 servings
Prep. Time: 30 minutes   Cooking Time: 6–8 hours   Ideal slow-cooker size: 5- or 6-qt.

3-lb. lean round steak
⅓ cup flour
2 tsp. kosher salt
½ tsp. black pepper
2 Tbsp. olive oil
1 large onion, or more, sliced
1 large bell pepper, or more, sliced
14½-oz. can low-sodium stewed tomatoes, or 3–4 fresh tomatoes, chopped
water

1. Cut meat into 10 pieces. Pound both sides. Mix together flour, salt, and pepper. Dredge each piece of meat on both sides in flavored flour.

2. Sauté meat in oil over medium heat in skillet, until browned. Transfer to slow cooker.

3. Brown onion and pepper in pan drippings. Add tomatoes and bring to boil. Stir pan drippings loose. Pour over steak. Add water to completely cover steak.

4. Cover. Cook on Low 6–8 hours.

Variations:

To add some flavor, stir your favorite dried herbs into Step 3. Or add fresh herbs just before serving.

Calories: 190
Fat: 7g
Sodium: 510mg
Carbs: 7g
Sugar: 3g
Protein: 23g

Slow-Cooker Beef Stroganoff

Becky Fixel, Grosse Pointe Farms, MI

Makes 6–8 servings

Prep. Time: 10 minutes ⚘ *Cooking Time: 6 hours* ⚘ *Ideal slow-cooker size: 5-qt.*

1 cup nonfat plain Greek yogurt

8 oz. reduced-fat cream cheese

¼ cup condensed mushroom soup mix

1 medium onion, minced

¼ cup butter

1 lb. stew beef

⅛ tsp. paprika

8–10 oz. mushrooms, sliced

½ cup fat-free milk

1 tsp. salt

1 tsp. pepper

1. Mix yogurt, cream cheese, and mushroom soup mix in medium bowl.

2. Add all ingredients to your crock and mix well.

3. Cover and cook on Low for 6 hours. You may stir occasionally.

Calories: 331
Fat: 25g
Sodium: 508mg
Carbs: 6g
Sugar: 508g
Protein: 22g

Convenient Slow-Cooker Lasagna

Rachel Yoder, Middlebury, IN

Makes 6–8 servings

Prep. Time: 30–45 minutes ⚹ *Cooking Time: 4 hours* ⚹ *Ideal slow-cooker size: 6-qt.*

1 lb. extra-lean ground beef

29-oz. can tomato sauce

8-oz. pkg. lasagna noodles, uncooked, *divided*

4 cups shredded low-fat mozzarella cheese

1½ cups low-fat cottage cheese

1. Spray the interior of the cooker with nonstick spray.

2. Brown the ground beef in a large nonstick skillet. Drain off drippings.

3. Stir in tomato sauce. Mix well.

4. Spread one-fourth of the meat sauce on the bottom of the slow cooker.

5. Arrange ⅓ of the uncooked noodles over the sauce. If you wish, break them up so they fit better.

6. Combine the cheeses in a bowl. Spoon ⅓ of the cheeses over the noodles.

7. Repeat these layers twice.

8. Top with remaining meat sauce.

9. Cover and cook on Low 4 hours.

Calories: 515
Fat: 25g
Sodium: 1415mg
Carbs: 32g
Sugar: 5g
Protein: 48g

Meat Sauce for Spaghetti

Becky Fixel, Grosse Pointe Farms, MI

Makes 6–8 servings

Prep. Time: 20 minutes ❦ *Cooking Time: 8 hours* ❦ *Ideal slow-cooker size: 7-qt.*

2 Tbsp. olive oil

28-oz. can crushed tomatoes

28-oz. can tomato sauce

15-oz. can Italian stewed tomatoes

6-oz. can tomato paste

2–3 Tbsp. basil

2 Tbsp. oregano

2 Tbsp. brown sugar

2 Tbsp. garlic paste (or 2 medium cloves, peeled and minced)

2 lbs. extra-lean ground sirloin or lean ground turkey

1. Pour olive oil in the crock. Use a paper towel to rub it all around the inside.

2. Add all ingredients except ground sirloin or turkey. Stir together and put slow cooker on Low.

3. In a large skillet, brown your ground sirloin, and drain off any extra grease. Add this to your slow cooker.

4. Cook on Low for 8 hours.

Serving suggestion:
Serve over your favorite pasta.

Calories: 370
Fat: 17g
Sodium: 360mg
Carbs: 28.5g
Sugar: 19g
Protein: 29.5g

Goulash

Janie Steele, Moore, OK

Makes 8–10 servings
Prep. Time: 15 minutes & Cooking Time: 6 hours & Ideal slow-cooker size: 5-qt.

1 lb. extra-lean ground beef

1 pkg. low-sodium taco seasoning

2 cups water

15-oz. can low-sodium diced tomatoes

15-oz. can low-sodium tomato sauce

15-oz. can whole-kernel corn, drained

Salt and pepper, to taste

2 cups uncooked elbow macaroni

1. Brown meat in a skillet and drain.

2. Mix remaining ingredients except the macaroni together and pour into slow cooker.

3. Add elbow macaroni, then mix.

4. Cover and cook 6 hours on Low.

Calories: 215
Fat: 4g
Sodium: 358mg
Carbs: 31g
Sugar: 6g
Protein: 14g

Sloppy Joes

Hope Comerford, Clinton Township, MI

Makes 15–18 servings
Prep. Time: 25 minutes ♣ Cooking Time: 6–7 hours ♣ Ideal slow-cooker size: 6-qt.

1 ½ lbs. extra-lean ground beef

16 oz. ground turkey sausage

½ large red onion, chopped

½ green bell pepper, chopped

8-oz. can low-sodium tomato sauce

½ cup water

½ cup ketchup

¼ cup tightly packed brown sugar

2 Tbsp. apple cider vinegar

2 Tbsp. yellow mustard

1 Tbsp. Worcestershire sauce

1 Tbsp. chili powder

1 tsp. garlic powder

1 tsp. onion powder

¼ tsp. salt

¼ tsp. pepper

1. Brown the ground beef and sausage in a pan. Drain all grease.

2. While the beef and sausage are cooking, mix together the remaining ingredients in the crock.

3. Add the cooked beef and sausage to the crock and mix.

4. Cover and cook on Low for 6–7 hours.

Serving suggestion:
Serve on hamburger buns.

Calories: 134
Fat: 7g
Sodium: 221mg
Carbs: 6g
Sugar: 4g
Protein: 13g

BBQ Meatloaf

Marjorie Nolt, Denver, PA

Makes 10 servings

Prep. Time: 30 minutes & Cooking Time: 5–6 hours & Ideal slow-cooker size: 6-qt. oval

2 lbs. extra-lean ground beef

1 lb. lean ground turkey sausage

½ cup finely chopped onion

½ cup almond flour

1 tsp. sea salt

1 tsp. black pepper

1 tsp. garlic powder

2 large eggs

1 cup of your favorite barbecue sauce, *divided*

Calories: 268
Fat: 14g
Sodium: 519mg
Carbs: 5g
Sugar: 2g
Protein: 30g

1. Grease interior of slow-cooker crock.

2. Make a tinfoil sling for your slow cooker so you can lift the cooked meatloaf out easily. Begin by folding a strip of aluminum foil accordion-fashion so that it's about 1½–2 inches wide, and long enough to fit from the top edge of the crock, down inside and up the other side, plus a 2-inch overhang on each side of the cooker. Make a second strip exactly like the first.

3. Place the one strip in the crock, running from end to end. Place the second strip in the crock, running from side to side. The 2 strips should form a cross in the bottom of the crock.

4. In a large bowl, mix all ingredients together, except barbecue sauce. Mix well with your hands until fully combined.

5. Place loaf into crock, centering it where the 2 foil strips cross.

6. Cover. Cook on Low 3–4 hours.

7. Thirty minutes before end of cooking time, brush top and sides of loaf with about ⅓ cup barbecue sauce.

8. Use foil handles to lift meatloaf out of the crock and onto a serving platter. Let stand 10–15 minutes to allow meat to gather its juices.

9. Slice and serve with remaining barbecue sauce.

Mexican Meatloaf

Jennifer Freed, Rockingham, VA

Makes 4–6 servings
Prep. Time: 20 minutes ⚹ *Cooking Time: 5–7 hours* ⚹ *Ideal slow-cooker size: 3- to 4-qt.*

2 lbs. extra-lean ground beef

2 cups panko bread crumbs

1 cup shredded low-fat cheddar cheese

⅔ cup salsa

2 eggs, beaten

4 Tbsp. low-sodium taco seasoning

1. Combine all ingredients in large bowl; mix well.

2. Shape meat mixture into loaf and place in slow cooker.

3. Cover; cook on Low for 5–7 hours, or until internal temperature is 165°F.

Calories: 374

Fat: 15g

Sodium: 673mg

Carbs: 16g

Sugar: 2g

Protein: 41g

Ruth Ann's Meatloaf

Ruth Ann Hoover, New Holland, PA

Makes 4 servings
Prep. Time: 15 minutes ☙ Cooking Time: 8–9 hours ☙ Ideal slow-cooker size: 4-qt.

I egg

¼ cup nonfat milk

2 slices day-old whole wheat bread, cubed

¼ cup chopped onions

2 Tbsp. chopped green peppers

I tsp. salt

¼ tsp. pepper

I ½ lbs. extra lean ground beef or turkey

¼ cup ketchup

8 small red potatoes

4–6 medium carrots, cut in I-inch chunks

1. Beat together egg and milk.

2. Stir in bread cubes, onions, green peppers, salt, and pepper. Add beef and mix well.

3. Shape into loaf that is about an inch smaller in circumference than the inside of the slow cooker. Place loaf into slow cooker.

4. Spread top with ketchup.

5. Peel strip around the center of each potato. Place carrots and potatoes around meatloaf.

6. Cover. Cook on High 1 hour. Reduce heat to Low. Cook 7–8 hours longer.

Calories: 501
Fat: 16g
Sodium: 1001mg
Carbs: 47g
Sugar: 14g
Protein: 43g

Nutritious Meatloaf

Elsie Russett, Fairbank, IA

Makes 6 servings
Prep. Time: 10 minutes ⚜ *Cooking Time: 3–4 hours* ⚜ *Ideal slow-cooker size: 4-qt.*

1 lb. extra-lean ground beef
2 cups finely shredded cabbage
1 medium green pepper, diced
1 Tbsp. dried onion flakes
½ tsp. caraway seeds
1 tsp. sea salt

1. Combine all ingredients. Shape into loaf and place on rack in slow cooker.

2. Cover. Cook on High 3–4 hours.

Calories: 132
Fat: 6g
Sodium: 313mg
Carbs: 3g
Sugar: 2g
Protein: 16g

Slow-Cooked Cabbage Rolls

Rebecca Meyerkorth, Wamego, KS

Makes 8 servings
Prep. Time: 30–45 minutes ❧ *Cooking Time: 4–6 hours* ❧ *Ideal slow-cooker size: 3- or 4-qt.*

large head cabbage

¼ cup **Egg Beaters**

8-oz. can tomato sauce

¾ cup instant rice, uncooked

½ cup green bell pepper, chopped

½ cup (approx. 15) crushed low sodium, low-fat crackers

1 envelope low-sodium dry onion soup mix

1½ lbs. 95% lean ground beef

46-oz. can low-sodium vegetable juice

½ cup reduced-fat grated Parmesan cheese, *optional*

1. Cook whole head of cabbage in boiling water just until outer leaves begin to loosen. Pull off 16 large leaves. Drain well. (Use remaining leaves for another meal.)

2. Cut out thick veins from bottoms of reserved leaves.

3. Combine Egg Beaters, tomato sauce, rice, green pepper, cracker crumbs, and dry soup mix in a bowl.

4. Crumble beef over mixture and mix well.

5. Place approximately ¼ cup of mixture on each cabbage leaf.

6. Fold in sides, beginning from cut end.

7. Roll up completely to enclose meat.

8. Secure each roll with a toothpick.

9. Place cabbage rolls in 3- or 4-qt. slow cooker.

10. Pour vegetable juice over rolls.

11. Cover and cook on Low 4–6 hours, or until rice is fully cooked, or filling reaches 160°F.

12. Just before serving, sprinkle each roll with cheese, if you wish.

Calories: 280
Fat: 6g
Sodium: 630mg
Carbs: 33g
Sugar: 13g
Protein: 23g

Swedish Cabbage Rolls

Jean Butzer, Batavia, NY
Pam Hochstedler, Kalona, IA

Makes 6 servings
Prep. Time: 25 minutes   ♣   *Cooking Time: 7–9 hours*   ♣   *Ideal slow-cooker size: 2- to 4-qt.*

12 large cabbage leaves
1 egg, beaten
¼ cup fat-free milk
¼ cup finely chopped onions
1 tsp. sea salt
¼ tsp. pepper
1 lb. extra-lean ground beef, browned and drained
1 cup cooked brown rice
8-oz. can low-sodium tomato sauce
1 Tbsp. brown sugar
1 Tbsp. lemon juice
1 tsp. Worcestershire sauce

1. Immerse cabbage leaves in boiling water for about 3 minutes or until limp. Drain.

2. Combine egg, milk, onions, salt, pepper, beef, and rice. Place about ¼ cup meat mixture in center of each leaf. Fold in sides and roll ends over meat. Place in slow cooker.

3. Combine tomato sauce, brown sugar, lemon juice, and Worcestershire sauce. Pour over cabbage rolls.

4. Cover. Cook on Low 7–9 hours.

Calories: 193
Fat: 7g
Sodium: 529mg
Carbs: 14g
Sugar: 4g
Protein: 19g

Stuffed Green Peppers

Lois Stoltzfus, Honey Brook, PA

Makes 6 servings
Prep. Time: 20 minutes & Cooking Time: 3–8 hours & Ideal slow-cooker size: 5- to 6-qt.

6 large green peppers

1 lb. extra-lean ground beef, browned

2 Tbsp. minced onion

1 tsp. salt

⅛ tsp. garlic powder

2 cups cooked rice

15-oz. can low-sodium tomato sauce

¾ cup shredded low-fat mozzarella cheese

1. Cut peppers in half and remove seeds.

2. Combine all ingredients except peppers and cheese.

3. Stuff peppers with ground beef mixture. Place in slow cooker.

4. Cover. Cook on Low 6–8 hours, or on High 3–4 hours. Sprinkle with cheese during last 30 minutes.

Calories: 270
Fat: 9g
Sodium: 735mg
Carbs: 25g
Sugar: 6g
Protein: 23g

Stuffed Bell Peppers

Mary Puterbaugh, Elwood, IN

Makes 8 servings
Prep. Time: 20 minutes ⚜ *Cooking Time: 5–11 hours* ⚜ *Ideal slow-cooker size: 6- to 7-qt.*

2 lbs. extra-lean ground beef, lightly browned

1 large onion, chopped

1 cup cooked brown rice

2 eggs, beaten

½ cup nonfat milk

½ cup ketchup

dash hot pepper sauce

2 tsp. sea salt

½ tsp. pepper

8 large bell peppers, capped and seeded

1. Combine all ingredients except peppers. Gently pack mixture into peppers. Place in greased slow cooker.

2. Cover. Cook on Low 9–11 hours, or on High 5–6 hours.

Calories: 274
Fat: 10g
Sodium: 627mg
Carbs: 18g
Sugar: 8g
Protein: 28g

PORK

Savory Pork Roast

Mary Louise Martin, Boyd, WI

Makes 4–6 servings
Prep. Time: 15 minutes   Cooking Time: 3½–4½ hours   Ideal slow-cooker size: 6-qt. oval

4-lb. boneless pork butt roast
1 tsp. ground ginger
1 Tbsp. fresh minced rosemary
½ tsp. mace or nutmeg
1 tsp. coarsely ground black pepper
2 tsp. salt
2 cups water

1. Grease interior of slow-cooker crock.

2. Place roast in slow cooker.

3. In a bowl, mix spices and seasonings together. Sprinkle half on top of roast, pushing down on spices to encourage them to stick.

4. Flip roast and sprinkle with rest of spices, again, pushing down to make them stick.

5. Pour 2 cups water around the edge, being careful not to wash spices off meat.

6. Cover. Cook on Low 3½–4½ hours, or until instant-read meat thermometer registers 140°F when stuck into center of roast.

Calories: 480
Fat: 15g
Sodium: 1100mg
Carbs: .5g
Sugar: 0g
Protein: 81.5g

Pork Roast and Vegetables

Jenny R. Unternahrer, Wayland, IA

Makes 8–10 servings

Prep. Time: 15 minutes ☙ Cooking Time: 6–8 hours ☙ Ideal slow-cooker size: 5–qt.

3 Tbsp. olive oil

3–4-lb. boneless pork chuck roast, trimmed

salt and pepper, to taste

¼ cup flour

2 Tbsp. tomato paste

½ cup dry white wine

1½ cups low-sodium beef or chicken broth

1 Tbsp. Worcestershire sauce

1 medium onion, thinly sliced (more or less onions as you like)

handful baby carrots

2 small stalks celery, thinly sliced

3 cloves garlic, diced

½ tsp. dried thyme

small potatoes, quartered

1. Heat oil in pan (preferably not a nonstick). Sprinkle roast with salt and pepper. Sear roast on all sides until browned, approximately 10 minutes. Place in large slow cooker.

2. Add flour and tomato paste to pan and cook for 1 minute. Add wine, broth, and Worcestershire sauce, scraping the bits off the bottom of the pan.

3. Pour over roast. Mix vegetables, garlic, and dried thyme in bowl and add to crock.

4. Cover and cook for 6–8 hours on Low. Add quartered potatoes to liquid after 4 hours. Serve in bowl so you can ladle the gravy over the top.

TIP
If you use Yukon Gold potatoes; they will hold their shape.

Calories: 84

Fat: 14g

Sodium: 275mg

Carbs: 8g

Sugar: 2g

Protein: 26g

Carolina Pot Roast

Jonathan Gehman, Harrisonburg, VA

Makes 3–4 servings

Prep. Time: 20 minutes ⚜ *Cooking Time: 3 hours* ⚜ *Ideal slow-cooker size: 3-qt.*

3 medium-large sweet potatoes, peeled and cut into 1-inch chunks

¼ cup brown sugar

1-lb. pork roast

scant ¼ tsp. cumin

sea salt, to taste

water

1. Place sweet potatoes in bottom of slow cooker. Sprinkle brown sugar over potatoes.

2. Heat nonstick skillet over medium-high heat. Add roast and brown on all sides. Sprinkle meat with cumin and salt while browning. Place pork on top of potatoes.

3. Add an inch of water to the cooker, being careful not to wash the seasoning off the meat.

4. Cover and cook on Low 3 hours, or until meat and potatoes are tender but not dry or mushy.

Calories: 118
Fat: 8g
Sodium: 130mg
Carbs: 28g
Sugar: 13g
Protein: 23g

Easiest Ever BBQ Country Ribs

Hope Comerford, Clinton Township, MI

Makes 12 servings
Prep. Time: 5 minutes & Cooking Time: 8–10 hours & Ideal slow-cooker size: 6-qt.

4 lbs. boneless country ribs

sea salt and pepper, to taste

18-oz. bottle of your favorite low-sugar barbecue sauce

1. Place your country ribs into your crock and sprinkle them with salt and pepper on both sides.

2. Pour half the bottle of barbecue sauce on one side of the ribs. Flip them over and poor the other half of the barbecue sauce on the other side of your ribs. Spread it around.

3. Cover and cook on Low for 8–10 hours.

Calories: 446
Fat: 24g
Sodium: 413mg
Carbs: 18g
Sugar: 17g
Protein: 40g

Simple Shredded Pork Tacos

Jennifer Freed, Rockingham, AL

Makes 6 servings
Prep. Time: 5 minutes ❧ *Cooking Time: 8 hours* ❧ *Ideal slow-cooker size: 4-qt.*

2-lb. boneless pork roast
1 cup salsa
4-oz. can chopped green chilies
½ tsp. garlic salt
½ tsp. black pepper

1. Place all ingredients in slow cooker.

2. Cover; cook on Low 8 hours, or until meat is tender.

3. To serve, use 2 forks to shred pork.

Serving suggestion:
Serve with taco shells and your favorite taco fixings.

Calories: 20
Fat: 11g
Sodium: 483mg
Carbs: 5g
Sugar: 3g
Protein: 29g

CHICKEN/TURKEY

Parmesan Chicken

Karen Waggoner, Joplin, MO

Makes 8 servings
Prep. Time: 15 minutes   Cooking Time: 4–4½ hours   Ideal slow-cooker size: 4- or 5-qt.

8 boneless, skinless chicken breast halves (about 2 lbs.)

½ cup water

1 cup fat-free mayonnaise

½ cup grated fat-free Parmesan cheese

2 tsp. dried oregano

¼ tsp. black pepper

¼ tsp. paprika

1. Place chicken and water in slow cooker.

2. Cover. Cook on High 2 hours.

3. Mix remaining ingredients. Spread over chicken.

4. Cover. Cook on High 2–2½ hours.

Calories: 180
Fat: 4g
Sodium: 400mg
Carbs: 4g
Sugar: 2g
Protein: 28g

Chicken and Dumplings

Bonnie Miller, Louisville, OH

Makes 4 servings
Prep. Time: 20 minutes ⚬ Cooking Time: 3½–8½ hours ⚬ Ideal slow-cooker size: 4-qt.

2 lbs. boneless, skinless chicken breast halves

1¾ cups low-sodium chicken broth

2 low-sodium chicken bouillon cubes

2 tsp. salt

1 tsp. pepper

1 tsp. poultry seasoning

2 stalks celery, cut into 1-inch pieces

6 small carrots, cut into 1-inch chunks

Biscuits:

2 cups buttermilk biscuit mix

½ cup plus 1 Tbsp. milk

1 tsp. parsley

1. Arrange chicken in slow cooker.

2. Dissolve bouillon in broth in bowl. Stir in salt, pepper, and poultry seasoning.

3. Pour over chicken.

4. Spread celery and carrots over top.

5. Cover. Cook on Low 6–8 hours or on High 3–3½ hours, or until chicken is tender but not dry.

6. Combine biscuit ingredients in a bowl until just moistened. Drop by spoonfuls over steaming chicken.

7. Cover. Cook on High 35 minutes. Do not remove cover while dumplings are cooking. Serve immediately.

Calories: 568
Fat: 14g
Sodium: 2378mg
Carbs: 47g
Sugar: 6g
Protein: 60g

Easy Chicken and Dumplings

Annabelle Unternahrer, Shipshewana, IN

Makes 5–6 servings
Prep. Time: 25 minutes ⚓ *Cooking Time: 2½–3½ hours* ⚓ *Ideal slow-cooker size: 3- or 4-qt.*

1 lb. uncooked boneless, skinless chicken breasts, cut in 1-inch cubes

1 lb. frozen vegetables of your choice

1 medium-sized onion, diced

2 12-oz. jars fat-free low-sodium chicken broth, *divided*

1½ cups low-fat buttermilk biscuit mix

1. Combine chicken, vegetables, onion, and chicken broth (reserve ½ cup plus 1 Tbsp. broth) in slow cooker.

2. Cover. Cook on High 2–3 hours.

3. Mix biscuit mix with reserved broth until moistened. Drop by tablespoonfuls over hot chicken and vegetables.

4. Cover. Cook on High 10 minutes.

5. Uncover. Cook on High 20 minutes more.

Variation:

For a less brothy stew, add another ½ pound vegetables.

Calories: 330
Fat: 8g
Sodium: 600mg
Carbs: 31g
Sugar: 7g
Protein: 33g

Chicken and Dressing

Sharon Miller, Holmesville, OH

Makes 10–12 servings
Prep. Time: 30 minutes ❧ Cooking Time: 4¾–8¾ hours ❧ Ideal slow-cooker size: 6-qt.

12–13 cups slightly dry bread cubes
1–2 cups chopped onion
2 cups diced celery
4 Tbsp. butter, melted
1 tsp. poultry seasoning
½ tsp. dried thyme
1½ tsp. salt
½ tsp. pepper
3 cups shredded or diced cooked chicken
3 well-beaten eggs
3½–4½ cups low-sodium chicken broth

1. Place bread cubes in a large bowl.

2. Sauté onion and celery in melted butter. Stir in poultry seasoning, thyme, salt, and pepper.

3. Toss in the cooked chicken.

4. Pour entire chicken mixture over bread cubes and toss well together.

5. Add the eggs.

6. Stir in chicken broth to moisten. Pack lightly into slow cooker.

7. Cover and cook on High for 45 minutes. Reduce heat to Low and cook 4–8 hours.

Serving suggestion:
A green vegetable and cranberry sauce would make a nice accompaniment to this dish.

TIP
This dish is ideal for a Thanksgiving meal as it does not tie up the oven.

Calories: 200
Fat: 8g
Sodium: 677mg
Carbs: 15g
Sugar: 2g
Protein: 17g

Mexi Chicken Rotini

Jane Geigley, Lancaster, PA

Makes 6 servings
Prep. Time: 30 minutes & Cooking Time: 4½ hours & Ideal slow-cooker size: 4-qt.

1 cup water

3 cups partially cooked rotini

12-oz. pkg. frozen mixed vegetables

10-oz. can Ro*Tel diced tomatoes with green chilies

4-oz. can green chilies, undrained

4 cups shredded cooked chicken

1 cup low-fat shredded cheddar cheese

1. Combine all ingredients in slow cooker except shredded cheddar.

2. Cover and cook on Low for 4 hours.

3. Top with shredded cheddar, then let cook covered an additional 20 minutes or so, or until cheese is melted.

Calories: 363
Fat: 11g
Sodium: 412mg
Carbs: 25g
Sugar: 3g
Protein: 38g

Moist and Tender Turkey Breast

Marlene Weaver, Lititz, PA

Makes 12 servings
Prep. Time: 10 minutes & Cooking Time: 4–6 hours & Ideal slow-cooker size: 6- or 7-qt.

1 bone-in turkey breast (6–7 lbs.)
4 fresh rosemary sprigs
4 cloves garlic, peeled
1 Tbsp. brown sugar
½ tsp. coarsely ground pepper
¼ tsp. salt

1. Place turkey in a crock and place rosemary and garlic around it.

2. Combine the brown sugar, pepper, and salt; sprinkle over turkey.

3. Cover and cook on Low for 4–6 hours or until turkey is tender.

Calories: 300
Fat: 13.25g
Sodium: 160mg
Carbs: 1.5g
Sugar: 1g
Protein: 41.5g

Traditional Turkey Breast

Hope Comerford, Clinton Township, MI

Makes 10–12 servings

Prep. Time: 10 minutes ⚘ *Cooking Time: 8 hours* ⚘ *Ideal slow-cooker size: 7-qt.*

7-lb. or less turkey breast

2 Tbsp. olive oil

Rub:

2 tsp. garlic powder

1 tsp. onion powder

1 tsp. salt

¼ tsp. pepper

1 tsp. poultry seasoning

1. Remove gizzards from turkey breast, rinse it, and pat dry. Place breast into crock.

2. Rub turkey breast all over with olive oil.

3. Mix together all rub ingredients. Rub this mixture all over turkey breast and press it in.

4. Cover and cook on Low for 8 hours.

Calories: 279
Fat: 9g
Sodium: 1327mg
Carbs: 3g
Sugar: 2g
Protein: 49g

Kielbasa and Cabbage

Mary Ann Lefever, Lancaster, PA

Makes 4 servings
Prep. Time: 10–15 minutes 🍀 Cooking Time: 8 hours 🍀 Ideal slow-cooker size: 4- or 5-qt.

1 lb. turkey kielbasa, cut into 4 chunks

4 large white potatoes, cut into chunks

1-lb. head green cabbage, shredded

1 qt. whole tomatoes (strained if you don't like seeds)

onion, thinly sliced, *optional*

1. Layer kielbasa, then potatoes, and then cabbage into slow cooker.

2. Pour tomatoes over top.

3. Top with sliced onion if you wish.

4. Cover. Cook on High 8 hours, or until meat is cooked through and vegetables are as tender as you like them.

TIP
If desired, brown kielbasa in a skillet over medium heat before adding to slow cooker.

Calories: 316
Fat: 10g
Sodium: 1368mg
Carbs: 35g
Sugar: 11g
Protein: 25g

Turkey Lasagna with Homemade Sauce

Hope Comerford, Clinton Township, MI

Makes 8 servings
Prep. Time: 30 minutes   ⚬   Cooking Time: 3 hours   ⚬   Ideal slow-cooker size: 6-qt.

1 lb. lean ground turkey

1 medium onion, chopped

salt and pepper, to taste

28-oz. can crushed tomatoes

15-oz. can tomato sauce

2 tsp. Italian seasoning

1 tsp. garlic powder

1 tsp. onion powder

1 cup skim ricotta cheese

1½ cups low-fat shredded mozzarella cheese, *divided*

6–8 lasagna noodles, uncooked, *divided*

½ cup low-fat shredded Parmesan cheese

1. Spray crock well with nonstick spray.

2. Brown turkey with onion. Season with salt and pepper.

3. Add the crushed tomatoes, tomato sauce, Italian seasoning, garlic powder, and onion powder to the browned turkey/onion mixture and simmer on Low for about 5 minutes.

4. While the sauce is simmering, mix together the 1 cup ricotta cheese and 1 cup of the shredded mozzarella cheese. Set aside.

5. In the bottom of your crock, add ⅓ of the sauce.

6. Line the bottom of the crock with about 3 noodles.

7. Spread half of the ricotta/mozzarella mixture over the noodles and add ⅓ of the sauce again.

8. Add another layer of noodles, ricotta/mozzarella mixture, and remaining sauce.

9. Cook on Low for about 3 hours.

10. About 20 minutes before serving, sprinkle the top with remaining ½ cup mozzarella cheese and the Parmesan cheese.

Calories: 226
Fat: 5g
Sodium: 662mg
Carbs: 24g
Sugar: 6g
Protein: 22g

Turkey Lasagna

Rhoda Atzeff, Lancaster, PA

Makes 8–10 servings
Prep. Time: 20–30 minutes ⚬ *Cooking Time: 5 hours* ⚬ *Ideal slow-cooker size: 5-qt.*

1 lb. lean ground turkey

1 onion, chopped

⅛ tsp. garlic powder

2 15-oz. cans low-sodium tomato sauce

6-oz. can low-sodium tomato paste

½–1 tsp. sea salt

1 tsp. dried oregano, or ½ tsp. dried oregano and ½ tsp. dried basil

12 oz. fat-free cottage cheese

½ cup grated Parmesan cheese

12 oz. shredded nonfat mozzarella cheese

12 oz. lasagna noodles, uncooked, *divided*

1. Brown ground turkey and onion in skillet. Drain off any drippings.

2. Stir garlic powder, tomato sauce, tomato paste, salt, and herbs into browned turkey in skillet.

3. In a good-sized mixing bowl, blend together cottage cheese, Parmesan cheese, and mozzarella cheese.

4. Spoon ⅓ of meat sauce into slow cooker.

5. Add ⅓ of uncooked lasagna noodles, breaking them to fit.

6. Top with ⅓ of cheese mixture. You may have to use a knife to spread it.

7. Repeat layers two more times.

8. Cover. Cook on Low 5 hours.

9. Allow to stand 10 minutes before serving.

Calories: 293
Fat: 2g
Sodium: 1168mg
Carbs: 39g
Sugar: 1168g
Protein: 31g

Now That's Lasagna

Shirley Unternahrer, Wayland, IA

Makes 10 servings
Prep. Time: 20 minutes   ❧   Cooking Time: 4 hours   ❧   Ideal slow-cooker size: 6-qt.

1 lb. ground turkey sausage

1 small onion, chopped

1 small bell pepper, chopped

1 qt. low-sodium tomato juice, *divided*

15 gluten-free lasagna noodles, uncooked, *divided*

12 oz. low-fat cottage cheese, *divided*

3 cups shredded low-fat mozzarella cheese, *divided*

28-oz. jar organic no-sugar-added spaghetti sauce of your choice, *divided*

6 oz. sliced turkey pepperoni

1. Brown sausage in skillet. Drain off the drippings. Add chopped onion and pepper to skillet. Sauté 3 minutes with meat.

2. Pour 1 cup tomato juice into slow cooker as first layer.

3. Add a layer of 5 uncooked lasagna noodles. Break to fit inside curved edges of slow cooker.

4. Spread with half of cottage cheese as next layer. Spoon half of meat/veggie mix over cottage cheese. Sprinkle with 1 cup mozzarella cheese. Spoon half of spaghetti sauce over grated cheese.

5. Add another layer of 5 lasagna noodles.

6. Add remaining cottage cheese, followed by a layer of remaining meat/veggie mix. Add remaining 5 noodles.

7. Top with pepperoni slices, remaining spaghetti sauce, and half of remaining mozzarella cheese. Pour rest of tomato juice slowly around edge of cooker and its ingredients.

8. Cover. Cook on High 3½ hours. Remove lid and top with remaining mozzarella cheese. Cook another 15 minutes.

9. Allow lasagna to rest 15–20 minutes before serving.

Calories: 496
Fat: 19g
Sodium: 1807mg
Carbs: 49g
Sugar: 8g
Protein: 37g

Turkey "Spaghetti" Quinoa

Hope Comerford, Clinton Township, MI

Makes 8–10 servings

Prep. Time: 10–15 minutes ⚜ *Cooking Time: 5 hours* ⚜ *Ideal slow-cooker size: 5- or 6-qt.*

2 lbs. lean ground turkey

½ tsp. salt

⅛ tsp. pepper

1 tsp. garlic powder

1 tsp. onion powder

1 cup quinoa

1 cup chopped onion

1 cup shredded mozzarella cheese
(for dairy-free, replace with dairy-free cheese or leave out)

4 cups tomato sauce

2 cups water

1. Brown turkey with the salt, pepper, garlic powder, and onion powder.

2. Spray crock with nonstick spray.

3. Place ground turkey in bottom of crock. Top with quinoa, onion, and shredded mozzarella.

4. Pour tomato sauce and water into crock. Stir so everything is mixed.

5. Cover and cook on Low for 5 hours.

Calories: 300
Fat: 12.5g
Sodium: 800mg
Carbs: 20.5g
Sugar: 5g
Protein: 26g

Turkey Slow-Cooker Pizza

Evelyn L. Ward, Greeley, CO
Ann Van Doren, Lady Lake, FL

Makes 8 servings
Prep. Time: 25 minutes ⚮ Cooking Time: 3 hours ⚮ Ideal slow-cooker size: 6-qt.

1½ lbs. 99% lean ground turkey

¼ cup chopped onions

1 Tbsp. olive oil

28-oz. jar fat-free, low-sodium spaghetti sauce

4½-oz. can sliced mushrooms, drained

1–1½ tsp. Italian seasoning, according to your taste preference

12-oz. pkg. wide egg noodles, slightly undercooked

2 cups fat-free, shredded mozzarella cheese

2 cups low-fat, low-sodium, shredded cheddar cheese

1. In a large skillet, cook turkey and onions in olive oil until turkey is no longer pink. Drain.

2. Stir in spaghetti sauce, mushrooms, and Italian seasoning.

3. Spray slow cooker with nonfat cooking spray. Spread ¼ of meat sauce in pot.

4. Cover with ⅓ of noodles. Top with ⅓ of cheeses.

5. Repeat layers twice.

6. Cover. Cook on Low 3 hours. Do not overcook.

TIP

You may create your own Italian seasoning by combining equal parts dried basil, oregano, rosemary, marjoram, thyme, and sage. Mix well. Stir in a tightly covered jar in a dry and dark place.

Calories: 360
Fat: 8g
Sodium: 1290mg
Carbs: 23g
Sugar: 8g
Protein: 48g

SEAFOOD AND MEATLESS

Shrimp Marinara

Jan Mast, Lancaster, PA

Makes 4–5 servings
Prep. Time: 10–15 minutes 🍂 Cooking Time: 6¼–7¼ hours 🍂 Ideal slow-cooker size: 4-qt.

6-oz. can low-sodium tomato paste

2 Tbsp. dried parsley

1 clove garlic, minced

¼ tsp. pepper

½ tsp. dried basil

1 tsp. dried oregano

scant ½ tsp. salt

scant ½ tsp. garlic powder

28-oz. can low-sodium diced tomatoes, *divided*

1 lb. cooked shrimp, peeled

1. In slow cooker, combine tomato paste, parsley, garlic, pepper, basil, oregano, salt, garlic powder, and half the can of diced tomatoes.

2. Cook on Low 6–7 hours.

3. Turn to High and add shrimp.

4. If you'd like the sauce to have more tomatoes, stir in remaining tomatoes.

5. Cover and cook an additional 15–20 minutes.

Serving suggestion:

Serve over cooked spaghetti squash, garnished with grated Parmesan cheese if you wish.

Calories: 171
Fat: 2g
Sodium: 1450mg
Carbs: 18g
Sugar: 11g
Protein: 24g

Baked Ziti

Hope Comerford, Clinton Township, MI

Makes 8 servings
Prep. Time: 15 minutes & Cooking Time: 4 hours & Ideal slow-cooker size: 5-qt.

28-oz. can low-sodium crushed tomatoes

15-oz. can low-sodium tomato sauce

1½ tsp. Italian seasoning

1 tsp. garlic powder

1 tsp. onion powder

1 tsp. pepper

1 tsp. sea salt

1 lb. ziti or rigatoni pasta, uncooked, *divided*

1–2 cups low-fat shredded mozzarella cheese, *divided*

1. Spray crock with nonstick spray.

2. In a bowl, mix together crushed tomatoes, tomato sauce, Italian seasoning, garlic powder, onion powder, pepper, and salt.

3. In the bottom of the crock, pour ⅓ of the pasta sauce.

4. Add ½ of the pasta on top of the sauce.

5. Add another ⅓ of your pasta sauce.

6. Spread ½ of the mozzarella cheese on top of that.

7. Add the remaining pasta, the remaining sauce, and the remaining cheese on top of that.

8. Cover and cook on Low for 4 hours.

Calories: 398
Fat: 11g
Sodium: 1054mg
Carbs: 54g
Sugar: 7g
Protein: 23g

Fresh Veggie Lasagna

Deanne Gingrich, Lancaster, PA

Makes 4–6 servings

Prep. Time: 30 minutes ♣ *Cooking Time: 4 hours* ♣ *Ideal slow-cooker size: 4- or 5-qt.*

1½ cups shredded low-fat mozzarella cheese

½ cup low-fat ricotta cheese

⅓ cup grated Parmesan cheese

1 egg, lightly beaten

1 tsp. dried oregano

¼ tsp. garlic powder

3 cups marinara sauce, *divided*

1 medium zucchini, diced, *divided*

4 uncooked lasagna noodles

4 cups fresh baby spinach, *divided*

1 cup fresh mushrooms, sliced, *divided*

1. Grease interior of slow-cooker crock.

2. In a bowl, mix together mozzarella, ricotta, and Parmesan cheeses, egg, oregano, and garlic powder. Set aside.

3. Spread ½ cup marinara sauce in crock.

4. Sprinkle with half the zucchini.

5. Spoon ⅓ of cheese mixture over zucchini.

6. Break 2 noodles into large pieces to cover cheese layer.

7. Spread ½ cup marinara over the noodles.

8. Top with half the spinach and then half the mushrooms.

9. Repeat layers, ending with cheese mixture, and then sauce. Press layers down firmly.

10. Cover and cook on Low for 4 hours, or until vegetables are as tender as you like them and noodles are fully cooked.

11. Let stand 15 minutes so lasagna can firm up before serving.

Calories: 260
Fat: 11g
Sodium: 690mg
Carbs: 25g
Sugar: 6.5g
Protein: 15.5g

Faked You Out Alfredo

Sue Hamilton, Benson, AZ

Makes 4 servings
Prep. Time: 5 minutes & Cooking Time: 6 hours & Ideal slow-cooker size: 3-qt.

1-lb. bag frozen cauliflower

13½-oz. can light coconut milk

½ cup diced onion

2 cloves garlic, minced

1 Tbsp. vegetable stock concentrate

Salt and pepper, to taste

1. Place the frozen cauliflower, coconut milk, onion, garlic, and the vegetable stock concentrate in your crock. Stir mixture to blend in the stock concentrate.

2. Cover and cook on Low for 6 hours.

3. Place cooked mixture in blender and process until smooth.

4. Add salt and pepper to taste.

Serving suggestion:
Serve over cooked pasta, cooked sliced potatoes, or any other vegetable.

TIP
My husband loves this on pasta with cooked mushrooms mixed in. This sauce can be made ahead of time and refrigerated.

Calories: 205
Fat: 5g
Sodium: 300mg
Carbs: 36g
Sugar: 7g
Protein: 7g

Slow-Cooker Mac and Cheese

Jessica Stoner, Plain City, OH

Makes 4–6 servings

Prep. Time: 15–20 minutes ❧ *Cooking Time: 3½ hours* ❧ *Ideal slow-cooker size: 3-qt.*

4 cups cooked gluten-free elbow macaroni (1 cup dry)

2 eggs, beaten

1 cup low-fat shredded mild cheddar cheese

2 cups low-fat shredded sharp cheddar cheese

12-oz. can low-fat or fat-free evaporated milk

½ cup fat-free milk

2 Tbsp. butter, melted, *optional*

1 tsp. sea salt

pinch pepper

1. Place cooked macaroni in slow cooker.

2. Mix all other ingredients in a separate bowl.

3. Pour over macaroni. Don't stir!

4. Cover and cook on Low for 3½ hours.

Calories: 350
Fat: 10g
Sodium: 745mg
Carbs: 38g
Sugar: 10g
Protein: 25g

Easy Mac 'n' Cheese

Juanita Weaver, Johnsonville, IL

Makes 6 servings
Prep. Time: 5 minutes   ⚮   Cooking Time: 1½–2 hours   ⚮   Ideal slow-cooker size: 4½-qt.

2 cups dry macaroni

4 cups nonfat milk

I tsp. sea salt

1–2 pinches black pepper

4 oz. reduced-fat cream cheese

8 oz. reduced-fat shredded cheddar cheese

½ tsp. dry mustard or I tsp. prepared mustard

2 Tbsp. butter

4 slices ham, cut into squares, *optional*

1. Measure all ingredients into slow cooker.

2. Turn cooker on High.

3. Cover and cook for 30 minutes, then stir lightly to evenly distribute cheeses.

4. Cook for another hour or so.

Calories: 348
Fat: 11g
Sodium: 704mg
Carbs: 38g
Sugar: 11g
Protein: 22g

Vegetable-Stuffed Peppers

Shirley Hinh, Wayland, IA

Makes 8 servings
Prep. Time: 20 minutes ⚬ Cooking Time: 6–8 hours ⚬ Ideal slow-cooker size: 6-qt.

4 large green, red, or yellow bell peppers

½ cup brown rice

¼ cup minced onions

¼ cup black olives, sliced

2 tsp. soy sauce or Bragg liquid aminos

¼ tsp. black pepper

1 clove garlic, minced

28-oz. can low-sodium whole tomatoes

6-oz. can low-sodium tomato paste

15¼-oz. can corn or kidney beans, drained

1. Cut tops off peppers (reserve) and remove seeds. Stand peppers up in slow cooker.

2. Mix remaining ingredients in a bowl. Stuff peppers. (You'll have leftover filling.)

3. Place pepper tops back on peppers. Pour remaining filling over the stuffed peppers and work down in between the peppers.

4. Cover and cook on Low 6–8 hours, or until the peppers are done to your liking.

5. If you prefer, you may add ½ cup tomato juice if recipe is too dry.

6. Cut peppers in half and serve.

Serving suggestion:

Drizzle with Greek yogurt.

Calories: 180
Fat: 2g
Sodium: 420mg
Carbs: 34g
Sugar: 11g
Protein: 8g

Side Dishes & Vegetables

Best Smashed Potatoes

Colleen Heatwole, Burton, MI

Makes 12 servings
Prep. Time: 30 minutes ☙ Cooking Time: 5–6 hours ☙ Ideal slow-cooker size: 5½-qt.

5 lbs. potatoes, cooked, peeled, mashed, or riced

8 ozs. reduced-fat cream cheese, at room temperature

1½ cups nonfat plain Greek yogurt, at room temperature

¾ tsp. garlic salt or onion salt

1½ tsp. salt

¼ tsp. pepper

2 Tbsp. butter, *optional*

1. Combine all ingredients in slow cooker.

2. Cover. Cook on Low 5–6 hours.

Calories: 185
Fat: 3g
Sodium: 440mg
Carbs: 33g
Sugar: 5g
Protein: 9g

Parmesan Potato Wedges

Carol and John Ambrose, McMinnville, OR

Makes 6 servings

Prep. Time: 15 minutes   ⚬   Cooking Time: 4 hours   ⚬   Ideal slow-cooker size: 3-qt.

2 lbs. red potatoes, cut into ½-inch wedges or strips

¼ cup chopped onion

2 Tbsp. butter, cut into pieces

1½ tsp. dried oregano

¼ cup grated Parmesan cheese

1. Layer potatoes, onion, butter, and oregano in slow cooker.

2. Cover and cook on High 4 hours, or until potatoes are tender but not dry or mushy.

3. Spoon into serving dish and sprinkle with cheese.

Calories: 157
Fat: 5g
Sodium: 118mg
Carbs: 25g
Sugar: 2g
Protein: 4g

Lightened-Up Cheesy Potatoes

Hope Comerford, Clinton Township, MI

Makes 8–10 servings
Prep. Time: 10 minutes ❧ *Cooking Time: 4–5 hours* ❧ *Ideal slow-cooker size: 4-qt.*

32-oz. bag frozen gluten-free shredded hash browns

1 cup diced onions

8 oz. low-fat shredded cheddar cheese

1 cup nonfat plain Greek yogurt

1 cup nonfat milk

1 cup low-sodium chicken stock

3 oz. reduced-fat cream cheese

1 tsp. garlic powder

1 tsp. onion powder

1 tsp. kosher salt

¼ tsp. ground black pepper

1. Spray crock with nonstick cooking spray.

2. Place all frozen shredded hash browns in crock.

3. In a medium bowl, mix the remaining ingredients. Pour this over the hash browns and mix well in the crock.

4. Cover and cook on Low for 4–5 hours.

Calories: 157
Fat: 5g
Sodium: 118mg
Carbs: 25g
Sugar: 2g
Protein: 4g

Scalloped Potatoes

Hope Comerford, Clinton Township, MI

Makes 10–12 servings
Prep. Time: 25 minutes ⚭ Cooking Time: 5 hours
Standing Time: 15–20 minutes ⚭ Ideal slow-cooker size: 6- or 7-qt.

1 cup nonfat plain Greek yogurt

1 cup reduced-sodium chicken stock
or vegetable stock

1 Tbsp. salted butter, melted

4 Tbsp. flour

3 cloves garlic, minced

1 Tbsp. chopped fresh thyme

½ tsp. dry ground mustard

1 tsp. sea salt

¼ tsp. pepper

10 cups peeled and sliced
(about ⅛-inch thick) russet potatoes

½ cup chopped onion

8 oz. low-fat extra-sharp shredded
cheddar cheese

1. Spray crock well with nonstick cooking spray.

2. In a bowl, mix together the yogurt, chicken stock, butter, flour, garlic, dry ground mustard, sea salt, and pepper.

3. Arrange ⅓ of the potatoes on the bottom of the crock, overlapping each slightly. Sprinkle them with ⅓ of the chopped onions, ⅓ of the cheese, then pour ⅓ of the sauce you mixed in the bowl over the top. Repeat this process two more times.

4. Make sure the potatoes are submerged. Press them down if needed. Cover and cook on Low for 5 hours. Let stand for 15–20 minutes, or until thickened.

Calories: 170
Fat: 2g
Sodium: 269mg
Carbs: 34g
Sugar: 4g
Protein: 6g

German Potato Salad

Hope Comerford, Clinton Township, MI

Makes 6 servings
Prep. Time: 20 minutes ❧ Cooking Time: 5 hours ❧ Ideal slow-cooker size: 4-qt.

1½ lbs. red potatoes, coarsely chopped

1 medium onion, chopped

2 slices cooked turkey bacon, chopped

1 cup chopped celery

¼ cup apple cider vinegar

2 Tbsp. whole-grain mustard

1 Tbsp. olive oil

½ tsp. sea salt

¼ tsp. pepper

1 Tbsp. cornstarch

1. Place potatoes, onion, bacon, and celery in crock.

2. In a small bowl, combine the apple cider vinegar, mustard, olive oil, salt, pepper, and cornstarch. Pour this over the contents of the crock and stir.

3. Cover and cook on Low for 5 hours or until potatoes are tender.

Calories: 137
Fat: 3g
Sodium: 338mg
Carbs: 22g
Sugar: 3g
Protein: 5g

"Baked" Sweet Potatoes

Hope Comerford, Clinton Township, MI

Makes 5 potatoes

Prep. Time: 2 minutes   Cooking Time: 4–5 hours   Ideal slow-cooker size: 5- or 6-qt.

5 sweet potatoes, pierced in several places with a fork or knife

1. Place sweet potatoes in slow cooker.

2. Cover and cook on Low for 4–5 hours, or until they are tender when poked with a fork or knife.

Calories: 110
Fat: 0g
Sodium: 70mg
Carbs: 26g
Sugar: 5.5g
Protein: 2g

Maple-Glazed Sweet Potatoes

Jan Mast, Lancaster, PA

Makes 8–10 servings

Prep. Time: 20 minutes   ⚭   Cooking Time: 3–4 hours   ⚭   Ideal slow-cooker size: 2-qt.

8–10 medium-sized sweet potatoes
½ tsp. salt
½ cup maple syrup
1 Tbsp. butter
1 Tbsp. flour
¼ cup water

1. Cook sweet potatoes in 2–3 inches water in a large saucepan until barely soft. Drain. When cool enough to handle, peel and slice into slow cooker.

2. While potatoes are cooking in the saucepan, combine remaining ingredients in a microwave-safe bowl.

3. Microwave on High for 1½ minutes. Stir. Repeat until glaze thickens slightly.

4. Pour glaze over peeled, cooked sweet potatoes in slow cooker.

5. Cover and cook on High 3–4 hours.

TIP
These potatoes pair wonderfully with pork dishes.

Calories: 165
Fat: 1g
Sodium: 188mg
Carbs: 37g
Sugar: 15g
Protein: 2g

Sweet Potato and Cranberry Casserole

Mary E. Wheatley, Mashpee, MA

Makes 6–8 servings

Prep. Time: 20–30 minutes ✦ *Cooking Time: 3–4 hours* ✦ *Ideal slow-cooker size: 4- to 6-qt.*

¼ cup freshly squeezed orange juice

2 Tbsp. butter

1 Tbsp. olive oil

¼ cup maple syrup

1 tsp. ground cinnamon

1 cup dried cranberries

salt

4 lbs. sweet potatoes, or yams, peeled and cut into 1-inch pieces

1. Place all ingredients except sweet potatoes in slow cooker. Mix together.

2. Cover. Cook on High while preparing sweet potatoes.

3. Add sweet potato pieces to warm mixture.

4. Cover. Cook on High 3–4 hours.

5. When sweet potatoes are soft, stir until they're mashed and then serve.

Calories: 283
Fat: 5g
Sodium: 148mg
Carbs: 58g
Sugar: 20g
Protein: 4g

Corn on the Cob

Donna Conto, Saylorsburg, PA

Makes 3–4 servings
Prep. Time: 10 minutes ♣ Cooking Time: 2–3 hours ♣ Ideal slow-cooker size: 5- or 6-qt.

6–8 ears corn (in husk)
½ cup water

1. Remove silk from corn, as much as possible, but leave husks on.

2. Cut off ends of corncobs so ears can stand in the cooker.

3. Add water.

4. Cover. Cook on Low 2–3 hours.

Calories: 160
Fat: 2g
Sodium: 30mg
Carbs: 34g
Sugar: 6g
Protein: 6g

Chili-Lime Corn on the Cob

Hope Comerford, Clinton Township, MI

Makes 6 servings
Prep. Time: 10 minutes ❧ Cooking Time: 4 hours ❧ Ideal slow-cooker size: 6-qt.

6 ears corn, shucked and cleaned

3 tsp. butter, at room temperature

2 Tbsp. freshly squeezed lime juice

1 tsp. lime zest

2 tsp. chili powder

1 tsp. salt

½ tsp. pepper

1. Tear off 6 pieces of aluminum foil to fit each ear of corn. Place each ear of corn on a piece of foil.

2. Mix together butter, lime juice, lime zest, chili powder, salt, and pepper.

3. Divide butter mixture evenly among six ears of corn and spread it over ears of corn. Wrap them tightly with foil so they don't leak.

4. Place the foil-wrapped ears of corn into crock. Cover and cook on Low for 4 hours.

Calories: 98
Fat: 3g
Sodium: 373mg
Carbs: 18g
Sugar: 6g
Protein: 3g

Lightly Sweet Cornbread

Hope Comerford, Clinton Township, MI

Makes 6 servings
Prep. Time: 10 minutes   ⚶   Cooking Time: 3½–4 hours   ⚶   Ideal slow-cooker size: 3-qt.

1 cup cornmeal

1 cup flour

⅓ cup sugar

2 tsp. baking powder

2 Tbsp. butter, melted

¼ cup canola oil

1 egg

1–2 Tbsp. honey

1 cup nonfat milk

¼ cup frozen corn, *optional*

1. In a bowl, mix the cornmeal, flour, sugar, and baking powder.

2. Next, add the melted butter, oil, egg, honey, and milk and mix it up.

3. Add the corn (if using) and stir again.

4. Grease your crock with nonstick spray and pour in the batter.

5. Cover and cook on Low for 3½–4 hours.

TIP

If you know your slow cooker really well, you might notice it has a "hot spot" on which it tends to cook faster. When making breads or desserts, it's a good idea to cover that hot spot with aluminum foil. It will help keep your bread or dessert from burning in that spot!

Calories: 367

Fat: 19g

Sodium: 723mg

Carbs: 37g

Sugar: 5g

Protein: 13g

Fresh Green Beans

Lizzie Ann Yoder, Hartville, OH

Makes 6–8 servings
Prep. Time: 20 minutes ❧ Cooking Time: 6–24 hours ❧ Ideal slow-cooker size: 4- to 5-qt.

¼ lb. turkey bacon pieces

2 lbs. fresh green beans, washed and cut into pieces or frenched

3–4 cups water

1 scant tsp. sea salt

1. If using bacon, cut it into squares and brown in nonstick skillet. When crispy, drain and set aside.

2. Place all ingredients in slow cooker. Mix together well.

3. Cover and cook on High 6–10 hours or on Low 10–24 hours, or until beans are done to your liking.

Calories: 93
Fat: 4g
Sodium: 520mg
Carbs: 9g
Sugar: 4g
Protein: 6g

Cheesy Broccoli Casserole

Dorothy VanDeest, Memphis, TN

Makes 6 servings

Prep. Time: 10 minutes ⚜ *Cooking Time: 3–5 hours* ⚜ *Ideal slow-cooker size: 3-qt.*

10-oz. pkg. frozen chopped broccoli

6 eggs, beaten

24-oz. carton fat-free small-curd cottage cheese

6 Tbsp. flour

8 oz. fat-free mild cheese of your choice, diced

2 green onions, chopped

½ tsp. salt

1. Place frozen broccoli in colander. Run cold water over it until it thaws. Separate into pieces. Drain well.

2. Combine remaining ingredients in large bowl and mix until well blended. Stir in broccoli. Pour into slow cooker sprayed with fat-free cooking spray.

3. Cover. Cook on High 1 hour. Stir well, then resume cooking on Low 2–4 hours.

Variation:

You can use fresh broccoli instead of frozen.

Calories: 250
Fat: 4.5g
Sodium: 980mg
Carbs: 20g
Sugar: 8g
Protein: 32g

Slow-Cooker Beans & Rice

Kris Zimmerman, Lititz, PA

Makes 6–8 servings
Prep. Time: 15 minutes ♣ *Cooking Time: 3–4 hours* ♣ *Ideal slow-cooker size: 3-qt.*

3 cups cooked beans of your choice, rinsed and drained

1 cup brown rice

14½-oz. can diced tomatoes

1 Tbsp. coconut oil, melted

salt, to taste

1 tsp. cumin

½ tsp. garlic powder

2 cups water

diced green chilies, to taste, *optional*

hot sauce or cayenne pepper, to taste, *optional*

1. Place all ingredients in slow cooker and stir well.

2. Cover and cook on High for 3–4 hours. Begin checking at 3–3½ hours to see if your rice is done.

Calories: 240
Fat: 3.5g
Sodium: 110mg
Carbs: 44.5g
Sugar: 3g
Protein: 9.5g

Aunt Twila's Beans

Mary Louise Martin, Boyd, WI

Makes 10–12 servings

Prep. Time: 15 minutes ♣ Cooking Time: 10 hours ♣ Ideal slow-cooker size: 5-qt.

5 cups dry pinto beans

2 tsp. ground cumin

1 medium yellow onion, minced

4 cloves garlic, minced

9 cups water

3 tsp. salt

3 Tbsp. lemon juice

1. Combine beans, cumin, onion, garlic, and water in slow cooker.

2. Cook on Low for 8 hours.

3. Add salt and lemon juice. Stir. Cook on Low for another 2 hours.

Calories: 310
Fat: 1g
Sodium: 650mg
Carbs: 56.5g
Sugar: 2.5g
Protein: 19g

Desserts

Upside-Down Apple "Pie"

Hope Comerford, Clinton Township, MI

Makes 6 servings
Prep. Time: 15 minutes ☙ *Cooking Time: 6 hours* ☙ *Ideal slow-cooker size: 6-qt.*

8 Gala apples, peeled, cored, and sliced

1 ½ tsp. apple pie spice

¾ cup fat-free milk

½ cup turbinado sugar

2 eggs

1 ½ cups Bisquick, *divided*

5 Tbsp. coconut oil, *divided*

1 ½ tsp. vanilla extract

¼ cup brown sugar

1. Line the crock with parchment paper and spray with nonstick spray.

2. Place the apples and apple pie spice into the crock and stir.

3. In a medium-sized bowl, mix together the milk, turbinado sugar, eggs, ½ cup Bisquick, 2 Tbsp. of melted coconut oil, and the vanilla. Pour this over the apples.

4. In a small bowl, mix together the remaining Bisquick, coconut oil, and the brown sugar. It will be crumbly. Sprinkle this evenly over the contents of the crock.

5. Secure the lid of the slow cooker with some paper towels under it to absorb moisture.

6. Cook on Low for 6 hours.

Calories: 427
Fat: 17g
Sodium: 412mg
Carbs: 66g
Sugar: 38g
Protein: 6g

Low-Fat Apple Cake

Sue Hamilton, Minooka, IL

Makes 8 servings
Prep. Time: 20 minutes ⚶ *Cooking Time: 2½–3 hours* ⚶ *Ideal slow-cooker size: 4-qt.*

1 cup flour
¾ cup sugar
2 tsp. baking powder
1 tsp. ground cinnamon
¼ tsp. salt
4 medium-sized cooking apples, chopped
⅓ cup Egg Beaters
2 tsp. vanilla extract

1. Combine flour, sugar, baking powder, cinnamon, and salt.

2. Add apples, stirring lightly to coat.

3. Combine Egg Beaters and vanilla. Add to apple mixture. Stir until just moistened. Spoon into lightly greased slow cooker.

4. Cover. Bake on High 2½–3 hours.

5. Serve warm.

Calories: 180
Fat: 1g
Sodium: 85mg
Carbs: 41g
Sugar: 26g
Protein: 3g

Baked Apples with Dates

Mary E. Wheatley, Mashpee, MA

Makes 8 servings
Prep. Time: 20–25 minutes ♨ Cooking Time: 2–6 hours ♨ Ideal slow-cooker size: 6-qt. oval, or large enough cooker that the apples can each sit on the floor of the cooker, rather than being stacked

8 medium-sized baking apples

Filling:
¾ cup coarsely chopped dates
3 Tbsp. chopped pecans
¼ cup, or less, brown sugar

Topping:
1 tsp. ground cinnamon
½ tsp. ground nutmeg
1 Tbsp. butter

½ cup water

1. Wash, core, and peel top third of apples.

2. Mix dates and chopped pecans with small amount of brown sugar. Stuff into centers of apples where cores had been.

3. Set apples upright in slow cooker.

4. Sprinkle with cinnamon and nutmeg. Dot with butter.

5. Add water around inside edge of cooker.

6. Cover. Cook on Low 4–6 hours or on High 2–3 hours, or until apples are as tender as you like them.

Calories: 120
Fat: 2g
Sodium: 0mg
Carbs: 26g
Sugar: 23g
Protein: 1g

Healthy Coconut Apple Crisp

Hope Comerford, Clinton Township, MI

Makes 8–9 servings
Prep. Time: 20 minutes ॐ Cooking Time: 2 hours ॐ Ideal slow-cooker size: 3- or 4-qt.

5 medium Granny Smith apples, peeled, cored, sliced

1 Tbsp. cinnamon

¼ tsp. nutmeg

1 tsp. vanilla extract

Crumble:

1 cup oats

½ cup coconut flour

½ cup unsweetened coconut flakes

1 tsp. cinnamon

⅛ tsp. nutmeg

½ tsp. sea salt

2 Tbsp. honey

2 Tbsp. coconut oil, melted

2–3 Tbsp. unsweetened coconut milk

1. Spray crock with nonstick spray

2. In the crock, combine apple slices, cinnamon, nutmeg, and vanilla.

3. In a medium bowl, combine all of the crumble ingredients. If too dry, add a bit more honey or coconut milk. Pour over top of apple mixture.

4. Cover slow cooker and cook on Low for 2 hours.

Serving suggestion:
Serve with a scoop of coconut ice cream.

Calories: 240
Fat: 8.5g
Sodium: 230mg
Carbs: 38.5g
Sugar: 18.5g
Protein: 5g

Strawberry Rhubarb Crisp

Hope Comerford, Clinton Township, MI

Makes 6–8 servings
Prep. Time: 30 minutes ⚬ Cooking Time: 2–3 hours ⚬ Ideal slow-cooker size: 2½-qt.

Filling:

1 lb. strawberries, quartered if medium or large

3 rhubarb stalks, halved and sliced

¼ cup turbinado sugar

2 Tbsp. flour

2 tsp. vanilla extract

Crisp:

¼ cup turbinado sugar

2 Tbsp. flour

½ tsp. cinnamon

pinch salt

2 Tbsp. cold unsalted butter, sliced

½ cup old-fashioned oats

2 Tbsp. chopped pecans

2 Tbsp. chopped almonds

1. Spray your crock with nonstick spray.

2. Place the strawberries and rhubarb into the crock.

3. In a bowl, mix together the sugar, flour, and vanilla. Pour this over the strawberries and rhubarb and stir to coat evenly.

4. In another bowl, start on the crisp. Mix together the sugar, flour, cinnamon, and salt. Cut the butter in with a pastry cutter.

5. Stir in the oats, pecans, and almonds. Pour this mixture over the contents of the crock.

6. Cover and cook on Low for 2–3 hours.

7. The last half hour of cooking, remove the lid to help the crisp thicken.

Serving suggestion:

Serve over vanilla ice cream or on yogurt.

Calories: 138
Fat: 6g
Sodium: 2mg
Carbs: 21g
Sugar: 11g
Protein: 2g

Slow-Cooker Berry Cobbler

Wilma Haberkamp, Fairbank, IA
Virginia Graybill, Hershey, PA

Makes 8 servings
Prep. Time: 15–20 minutes 🔹 Cooking Time: 2–2½ hours 🔹 Ideal slow-cooker size: 5-qt.

1¼ cups all-purpose flour, *divided*

2 Tbsp. sugar, plus 1 cup sugar, *divided*

1 tsp. baking powder

¼ tsp. ground cinnamon

1 egg, lightly beaten

¼ cup skim milk

2 Tbsp. canola oil

⅛ tsp. salt

2 cups unsweetened raspberries, fresh, or thawed if frozen, and drained

2 cups unsweetened blueberries, fresh, or thawed if frozen, and drained

1. In mixing bowl, combine 1 cup flour, 2 Tbsp. sugar, baking powder, and cinnamon.

2. In a separate bowl, combine egg, milk, and oil. Stir into dry ingredients until moistened. Batter will be thick.

3. Spray slow cooker with cooking spray. Spread batter evenly on bottom of slow cooker.

4. In another bowl combine salt, remaining flour, remaining sugar, and berries. Toss to coat berries.

5. Spread berries over batter.

6. Cook on High 2–2½ hours, or until toothpick inserted into cobbler comes out clean.

TIP
If your diet permits, eat in soup bowl with cold milk poured over the top.

Calories: 260
Fat: 4.5g
Sodium: 50mg
Carbs: 52g
Sugar: 34g
Protein: 3g

Quick Yummy Peaches

Willard E. Roth, Elkhart, IN

Makes 6 servings
Prep. Time: 5–20 minutes ⚘ *Cooking Time: 5 hours* ⚘ *Ideal slow-cooker size: 3-qt.*

⅓ cup low-fat baking mix
⅔ cup oats
⅓ cup maple syrup
I tsp. ground cinnamon
4 cups sliced fresh peaches
½ cup water

1. Mix together baking mix, oats, maple syrup, and cinnamon in greased slow cooker.

2. Stir in peaches and water.

3. Cook on Low for at least 5 hours. (If you like a drier cobbler, remove lid for last 15–30 minutes of cooking.)

Calories: 140
Fat: 1g
Sodium: 60mg
Carbs: 33g
Sugar: 20g
Protein: 2g

Homestyle Bread Pudding

Lizzie Weaver, Ephrata, PA

Makes 6 servings
Prep. Time: 10–15 minutes ⚬ Cooking Time: 2 3 hours
deal slow-cooker size: large enough to hold your baking insert

⅓ cup **Egg Beaters**

2¼ cups fat-free milk

½ tsp. ground cinnamon

¼ tsp. salt

⅓ cup maple syrup

1 tsp. vanilla extract

2 cups 1-inch bread cubes

½ cup raisins

1. Combine all ingredients in bowl. Pour into slow-cooker baking insert. Cover baking insert. Place on metal rack (metal) in bottom of slow cooker.

2. Pour ½ cup hot water into cooker around outside of insert.

3. Cover slow cooker. Cook on High 2–3 hours.

4. Serve pudding warm or cold.

Calories: 150
Fat: .5g
Sodium: 230mg
Carbs: 32g
Sugar: 23g
Protein: 6g

Coconut Rice Pudding

Hope Comerford, Clinton Township, MI

Makes 6 servings
Prep. Time: 5 minutes & Cooking Time: 2–2½ hours & Ideal slow-cooker size: 5- or 6-qt

2½ cups low-fat milk

14-oz. can light coconut milk

½ cup turbinado sugar

1 cup Arborio rice

1 stick cinnamon

1 cup dried cranberries, *optional*

1. Spray crock with nonstick spray.

2. In crock, whisk together the milk, coconut milk, and sugar.

3. Add in the rice and cinnamon stick.

4. Cover and cook on Low about 2–2½ hours, or until rice is tender and the pudding has thickened.

5. Remove cinnamon stick. If using cranberries, sprinkle some on top of each bowl of Coconut Rice Pudding.

Calories: 250
Fat: 4g
Sodium: 70mg
Carbs: 48g
Sugar: 22g
Protein: 4g

Lotsa Chocolate Almond Cake

Hope Comerford, Clinton Township, MI

Makes 10 servings

Prep. Time: 10 minutes ⚬ Cooking Time: 3 hours ⚬ Cooling Time: 30 minutes ⚬ Ideal slow-cooker size: 6-qt.

1 ½ cups almond flour

¾ cup turbinado sugar

⅔ cup cocoa powder

¼ cup chocolate protein powder

2 tsp. baking powder

¼ tsp. salt

½ cup coconut oil, melted

4 eggs

¾ cup almond milk

1 tsp. vanilla extract

1 tsp. almond extract

¾ cup dark chocolate chips

1. Cover any hot spot of your crock with aluminum foil, and spray crock with nonstick spray.

2. In a bowl, mix together the almond flour, sugar, cocoa powder, protein powder, baking powder, and salt.

3. In a different bowl, mix together the coconut oil, eggs, almond milk, and vanilla and almond extracts.

4. Pour wet ingredients into dry ingredients and mix until well combined. Stir in chocolate chips.

5. Pour cake mix into crock. Cover and cook on Low for 3 hours.

6. Turn the slow cooker off when the cooking time is over and let the cake cool in the crock for 30 minutes.

7. Place a plate or platter over the crock, then turn the crock upside down on the plate, so the cake releases onto the plate or platter.

Calories: 338

Fat: 26g

Sodium: 117mg

Carbs: 22g

Sugar: 13g

Protein: 10g

Fudgy Secret Brownies

Juanita Weaver, Johnsonville, IL

Makes 8 servings
Prep. Time: 10 minutes   ⚬   Cooking Time: 1½–2 hours   ⚬   Ideal slow-cooker size: 6- or 7-qt.

4 oz. unsweetened chocolate

¾ cup coconut oil

¾ cup frozen diced okra, partially thawed

3 large eggs

1½ cups xylitol or your choice of sweetener

1 teaspoon pure vanilla extract

¼ tsp. mineral salt

¾ cup coconut flour

½–¾ cup coarsely chopped walnuts or pecans, *optional*

1. Melt chocolate and coconut oil in small saucepan.

2. Put okra and eggs in blender. Blend until smooth.

3. Measure all other ingredients in mixing bowl.

4. Pour melted chocolate and okra over the dry ingredients and stir with fork just until mixed.

5. Pour into greased slow cooker.

6. Cover and cook on High for 1½–2 hours.

Calories: 450
Fat: 31.5g
Sodium: 130mg
Carbs: 35.5g
Sugar: 2g
Protein: 6.5g

Black Bean Brownies

Juanita Weaver, Johnsonville, IL

Makes 6–8 servings
Prep. Time: 5 minutes ☙ Cooking Time: 1–1½ hours ☙ Ideal slow-cooker size: 5- or 6-qt.

15-oz. can black beans, rinsed and drained

6 eggs

⅓ cup cocoa powder

1½ tsp. aluminum-free baking powder

½ tsp. baking soda

2 Tbsp. coconut oil

2 tsp. pure vanilla extract

⅓ cup Greek yogurt or cottage cheese

¾ cup xylitol or your choice of sweetener

¼ tsp. salt

1. Put all ingredients in a food processor or blender. Blend until smooth.

2. Pour into greased slow cooker.

3. Cover and cook for 1–1½ hours on High.

4. Cool in crock. For best taste, chill before serving.

Calories: 230
Fat: 8.5g
Sodium: 360mg
Carbs: 29g
Sugar: .5g
Protein: 11g

Metric Equivalent Measurements

If you're accustomed to using metric measurements, I don't want you to be inconvenienced by the imperial measurements I use in this book.

Use this handy chart, too, to figure out the size of the slow cooker you'll need for each recipe.

Weight (Dry Ingredients)

1 oz		30 g
4 oz	¼ lb	120 g
8 oz	½ lb	240 g
12 oz	¾ lb	360 g
16 oz	1 lb	480 g
32 oz	2 lb	960 g

Slow Cooker Sizes

1-quart	0.96 l
2-quart	1.92 l
3-quart	2.88 l
4-quart	3.84 l
5-quart	4.80 l
6-quart	5.76 l
7-quart	6.72 l
8-quart	7.68 l

Volume (Liquid Ingredients)

½ tsp.		2 ml
1 tsp.		5 ml
1 Tbsp.	½ fl oz	15 ml
2 Tbsp.	1 fl oz	30 ml
¼ cup	2 fl oz	60 ml
⅓ cup	3 fl oz	80 ml
½ cup	4 fl oz	120 ml
⅔ cup	5 fl oz	160 ml
¾ cup	6 fl oz	180 ml
1 cup	8 fl oz	240 ml
1 pt	16 fl oz	480 ml
1 qt	32 fl oz	960 ml

Length

¼ in	6 mm
½ in	13 mm
¾ in	19 mm
1 in	25 mm
6 in	15 cm
12 in	30 cm

Recipe and Ingredient Index

V

Vegetable-Stuffed Peppers, 271
Vegetarian Split Pea Soup, 103

W

walnuts
    Apple Oatmeal, 11
    Fudgy Secret Brownies, 327
    Granola in the Slow Cooker, 23
    Oatmeal Morning, 15
    Warm 'n Fruity, 19
Warm 'n Fruity, 19
White and Green Chili, 165
White Bean and Chicken Chili, 159
White Chili, 157
wine
    Chianti
        Chianti-Braised Short Ribs, 185
    white
        French Onion Soup, 101
        Pork Roast and Vegetables, 221
Wintertime Vegetable Chili, 171

Y

yogurt
    Best Smashed Potatoes, 275
    Black Bean Brownies, 329
    Chicken, Pumpkin and Chickpea Stew, 145
    Chili Chicken Stew with Rice, 141
    Creamy Potato Soup, 117
    Scalloped Potatoes, 281
    Slow-Cooker Beef Stroganoff, 191
    Slow-Cooker Yogurt, 29
    White and Green Chili, 165
    Wintertime Vegetable Chili, 171

Z

zucchini
    Fresh Veggie Lasagna, 263
Zucchini Stew, 139

About the Author

Hope Comerford is a mom, wife, elementary music teacher, blogger, recipe developer, public speaker, ALM Zone Fitness Motivator, Young Living Essential Oils essential oil enthusiast/educator, and published author. In 2013, she was diagnosed with a severe gluten intolerance and since then has spent many hours creating easy, practical, and delicious gluten-free recipes that can be enjoyed by both those who are affected by gluten and those who are not.

Growing up, Hope spent many hours in the kitchen with her Meme (grandmother), and her love for cooking grew from there. While working on her master's degree when her daughter was young, Hope turned to her slow cookers for some salvation and sanity. It was from there she began truly experimenting with recipes and quickly learned she had the ability to get a little more creative in the kitchen and develop her own recipes.

In 2010, Hope started her blog, *A Busy Mom's Slow Cooker Adventures* to simply share the recipes she was making with her family and friends. She never imagined people all over the world would begin visiting her page and sharing her recipes with others as well. In 2013, Hope self-published her first cookbook, *Slow Cooker Recipes 10 Ingredients or Less and Gluten-Free*, and then later wrote *The Gluten-Free Slow Cooker*.

Hope is thrilled to be working with Fix-It and Forget-It and to be representing such an iconic line of cookbooks. She is excited to bring her creativity to the Fix-It and Forget-It brand. Through Fix-It and Forget-It, Hope has written many books, including *Fix-It and Forget-It Lazy & Slow*, *Fix-It and Forget-It Healthy Slow Cooker Cookbook*, *Fix-It and Forget-It Favorite Slow Cooker Recipes for Mom*, *Fix-It and Forget-It Favorite Slow Cooker Recipes for Dad*, and *Fix-It and Forget-It Instant Pot Cookbook*. Hope lives in the city of Clinton Township, Michigan, near Metro Detroit, and is a Michigan native. She has been happily married to her husband and best friend, Justin, since 2008. Together they have two children, Ella and Gavin, who are her motivation, inspiration, and heart. In her spare time, Hope enjoys traveling, singing, cooking, reading books, spending time with friends and family, and relaxing.